It's Quilting Cats & Dogs

It's Quilting Cats & Dogs

Lynette Anderson

D&C

David and Charles

www.rucraft.com

With thanks to my dear Mum and Dad for allowing cats, dogs and textiles into my life from such an early age and providing me with lifelong inspiration.

Printed in China by RR Donnelley
for David & Charles
Brunel House, Newton Abbot, Devon

Publisher Ali Myer
Acquisitions Editors Jane Trollope and Cheryl Brown
Assistant Editor Juliet Lines
Project Editor Lin Clements
Design Manager Sarah Clark
Designer Mia Farrant
Photographer Sian Irvine
Production Controller Kelly Smith

David and Charles publish high quality books on a wide range of subjects.
For more great book ideas visit: www.rucraft.co.uk

contents

Introduction   6

Puppy Dog Sewing Collection   10
Kitty Cat in the Garden   26
Woof! Woof!   38
I Love My Cat   52
Best of Friends   66
Summer Holiday   78
Forever Friends   94

Materials and Equipment   102
Basic Techniques   104
Embroidery Stitches   110
Templates   112
Suppliers   127
About the Author   127
Acknowledgments   127
Index   127

introduction

Welcome to my world of dogs and cats – those endearing creatures that many of us share our lives with – and the inspiration for the needlecraft projects in this book. I cannot remember a time without cats and dogs, or without some form of sewing. Crafts and particularly textiles have played a big part in my life from the age of five when I learnt to embroider with my Grandmother as my teacher.

In our household we currently have one dog and three cats, who are our friends and constant companions. I love the way they follow me around the house and settle into chairs and on top of cupboards – anywhere as long as they are close to me.

There are many stitching delights that await you within the pages of this book, as well as the adventures of Hugo the dog, Felix the cat and their feathered friend Mr Bird. There is some really enjoyable patchwork and quilting, some charming appliqué motifs and a gorgeous array of embroidery designs that you will enjoy sewing, plus a few stitching techniques you may not have tried before, such as punch needle work.

The **Kitty Cat in the Garden** chapter shows you how to make a beautiful quilt which is really easy to piece together. The quilt is adorned with little stitched panels of a contented cat as she makes herself at home amid the warm and mellow colours. There is also a charming journal cover to make – perfect for all your sewing notes or to jot down stories of your cat or dog.

The **Puppy Dog Sewing Collection** features a cute puppy and little bird stitched in simple embroidery stitches on a lovely sewing bag, needle case and scissor keeper, which could be made as a set or as individual items to give as gifts for friends. The colours are stylish and contemporary but the designs lend themselves to any fabrics.

The **I Love My Cat** chapter celebrates all cats – free-roaming toms, home-loving tabbies and elegant pedigrees. A fabulous wall hanging tells everyone you are a cat lover and combines several techniques, including crazy patchwork, strip piecing and blanket stitch appliqué. A blue and tan colour scheme adds extra zing. Some sweet pincushions in the shape of a curled-up sleeping cat make quick and easy gifts.

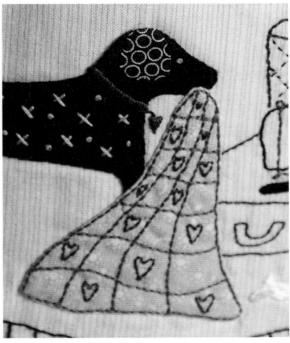

The **Woof! Woof!** chapter was inspired by my affection for my dog Hugo and the devoted work of the Seeing Eye dogs. The bed-sized quilt in this chapter is a combination of patchwork and appliqué. It's a real delight and destined to be much admired. There is also a wonderful dog-themed cushion that children will love.

The **Best of Friends** chapter features a really useful and roomy hand bag and a charming little purse. They were such fun to design and I'm sure you will love creating the crazy patchwork for the bag, which is quick and fun to do. I like to keep my coins in a separate purse and a little purse with some charming stitchery is the perfect size.

The **Summer Holiday** chapter was dreamt up whilst I lazed at our beach house. At Christmas, Easter and every weekend we can manage we escape there, loading the car up with all we need, plus our beloved furry friends. The lap quilt has easy nine-patch blocks and amusing scenes of Hugo, Felix and Mr Bird enjoying their holiday. A single stitched panel is used to decorate a stylish photo album.

The **Forever Friends** chapter celebrates the close companionship of Hugo and Felix in the sweetest little wall hanging created by punch needle embroidery, which is an old technique but really rewarding to do. A handy box showing Hugo with Mr Bird also uses the punch needle technique, and the idea could be used on the lid of any container.

The combination of patchwork, stitchery and appliqué is currently my favourite look and I hope you will enjoy it too. I love attention to detail but only use basic stitches, so my designs are achievable for all skill levels. All of the projects are described and illustrated with step-by-step instructions. Materials and equipment are described on page 102, followed by the basic techniques. Templates are on pages 112–126.

If you love dogs and cats, or know someone who does, or you simply love to sew something gorgeous and a touch quirky, then the charming projects in this book should bring you hours of stitching pleasure and satisfaction.

Enjoy
Lynette x.

puppy dog sewing collection

This lovely collection of sewing bag, needle case and scissor keeper is such fun to make and features charming stitched panels with quirky scenes of a puppy, little bird and sewing motifs. The embroideries are a delightful combination of needle-turn appliqué and surface embroidery stitches.

The collection was inspired by thoughts of a relaxing weekend away, with time to work on a sewing project. You could stitch all three as a collection for your own use or select just one project to make as a gift. I've chosen a black and white colour theme for the collection with touches of sage and red for contrast, creating a stylish yet appealing look.

The tote bag is big enough to hold a sewing project or other items. The needle case opens to reveal some useful pockets and a wool patch for pins and needles, while the scissor keeper uses thick card to create a rigid form to protect your scissors.

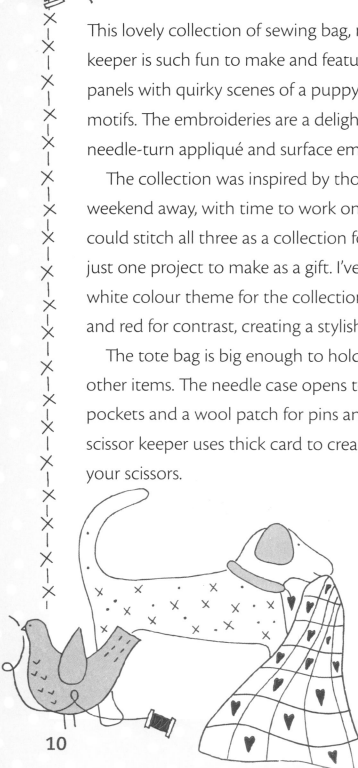

making the whole collection

You could make all three items in this sewing collection as a combined project or begin with one item and move on to the others afterwards. It is best to do the embroidery first as these pieces of fabric will be needed during the making up process for each project.

if making all the projects

Use the templates on pages 112–114 and transfer the stitchery designs for all the projects on to the right side of a 14in x 18in (36cm x 46cm) square of cream-on-cream print fabric, leaving at least 2in (5cm) between the designs to cut them apart later. Refer to page 104 for transferring designs. If using an iron-on stabilizer, use it before starting the stitching, following the manufacturer's instructions. You can do the appliqué on the bag before or after the stitchery has been completed – see page 15 for details.

if making individual projects

Follow the individual project instructions for the bag on page 14, the needle case on page 18 and the scissor keeper on page 22. Use the size of cream-on-cream print fabric given in the individual You Will Need lists.

working the embroidery

Once the designs are transferred on to your fabric you can begin working the stitches. I used two strands of DMC stranded cotton (unless otherwise stated). Colours used were country red (221), black (310), dirty green (3011), lime green (3819) and blanc (white). Stitches used were (abbreviations in brackets): backstitch (BS), satin stitch (SS), running stitch (RS), cross stitch (CS), lazy daisy (LD) and French knots (FK). See page 110 for how to work the various stitches. When all stitching is complete make the projects as described on page 14–25.

key for threads and stitches

 DMC 221 (country red)
Dog's collar (SS)
Hearts on quilt on bag (BS)
Heart on sewing machine (SS)
Dog's heart tag on bag (SS)
Suitcase (BS)
Thread trails and spools in all birds' mouths (BS & SS)
Sun (start in centre with FK then BS)
Sun rays (RS)
X's on needle case quilt (CS)

 DMC 310 (black)
Sewing machine outline (BS)
Sewing machine base (SS)
Lid of suitcase (RS, one strand)
All birds' eyes (FK)
All birds' legs (BS)
Outline of dog on needle case (BS)
X's and dots on needle case dog (CS & FK)
Tape measure (BS)
Numbers on tape measure (BS, one strand)
Outer border on needle case and scissor keeper (RS)
X's on outer borders (CS)
Spools, tops and bottoms (BS)
Name inside needle case (BS) – use the template on page 114 to create your name

 DMC 3011 (dirty green)
Lines on quilt, bag and needle case (BS)
Thread on sewing machine spool (BS & SS)
Thread coming out of suitcase (BS & FK)
Markings on appliqué bird's chest and tail (BS & RS)
Under hill on needle case (RS)

 DMC 3819 (lime green)
Markings on birds' chest and tail on scissor keeper and needle case outer and pocket (BS & RS)

 DMC Blanc (white)
Dog's bone on bag (SS)

sewing bag

This cute black puppy on this gorgeous bag is eagerly helping to pack the suitcase ready for a stitching weekend away. Not too big and not too small, the bag would make an ideal gift for a friend. The stitched panel on the front is charming and very rewarding to do.
Finished size (excluding handles) 12 x 9½in (30.5 x 24cm) approximately.

You will need...

- 12in (30cm) squares of four coordinating prints

- 8 x 12in (20 x 30cm) cream-on-cream print for stitchery

- 11 x 14in (28 x 35.5cm) print for back of bag

- Two 11 x 14in (28 x 35.5cm) pieces of lining fabric

- Scrap of dark cream print for appliqué quilt on bag

- Scraps of lime green print for appliqué bird on bag

- Scrap of black wool for dog

- 12in (30cm) square of iron-on stabilizer (optional)

- DMC stranded cotton: country red (221), dirty green (3011), lime green (3819), black (310) and blanc (white)

- 12in (30cm) square of lightweight iron-on wadding (batting) or pellon for bag

- Template plastic

- Fine-tipped fabric marking pen in brown

working the stitchery and appliqué

1 Using the stitchery template on page 113, transfer the stitchery designs for the bag on to the right side of the cream-on-cream print. Iron on the fusible stabilizer now, if using. Follow the instructions on page 12 for working the embroidery.

2 You can do the appliqué on the bag before or after the stitchery has been completed – I prefer to do mine before. Use the appliqué templates on page 112 and your favourite method of appliqué (see page 105 for guidance), apply the bird, its wing, the quilt, the dog and his ear on to the bag piece. If using a needle-turn appliqué method as I did, add a ¼in (6mm) seam allowance to the appliqué shapes. If using fusible web appliqué no seam allowance is needed. The dog will not need a seam allowance as wool does not fray. Add the surface stitches to the appliqués as described in the stitches key on page 12.

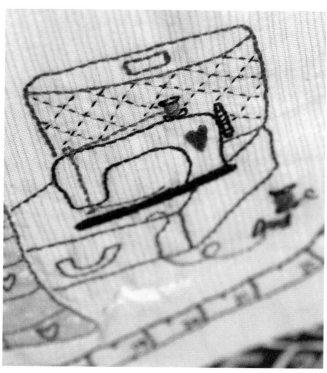

making the bag

3 Once all the appliqué and embroidery has been completed, carefully press your work. Trim the fabric to 10½ x 7in (26.7 x 18cm).

4 Using the templates on page 112 and template plastic, make templates of the scalloped top edge and the bottom section of the bag. From your chosen fabrics cut one from the scalloped top edge template and one from the bottom section template adding a ¼in (6mm) seam allowance all round. Clip all curves on the scalloped top edge piece and tack (baste) under the ¼in (6mm) seam allowance (see Fig 1). Press well.

FIG 1

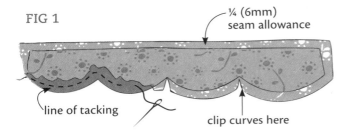

¼ (6mm) seam allowance

line of tacking

clip curves here

5 Pin the scalloped piece to the top of the embroidered panel and stitch in place along the scalloped edge using a blind hem stitch. Press gently.

6 Add the fabric piece for the bottom section to the stitched panel by pinning them right sides together, with straight edges aligned (Fig 2). Machine stitch along the straight edge using a ¼in (6mm) seam. Press the seam to the bottom section.

7 Using the bag front as a template cut this shape from the fabric you want on the back of your bag and then cut two from the fabric you are using for your bag lining and two from the lightweight iron-on wadding (batting).

> **TIP**
> If you wish, you could make a pieced back for your bag, matching the shapes used on the front.

8 Following the manufacturer's instructions, iron the lightweight iron-on wadding to the wrong side of the front and back of the bag outer. Take the front and the back of the bag and pin right sides together, and then stitch together using a ¼in (6mm) seam, leaving the top open (Fig 3).

9 Repeat this process for the bag lining but leave approximately 3in (7.5cm) of one seam open, so once the bag is almost completed you can turn it through this opening to the right side.

FIG 3

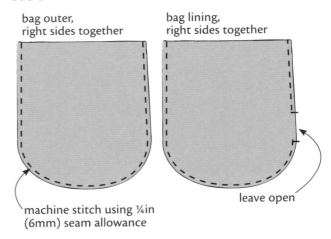

bag outer, right sides together

bag lining, right sides together

machine stitch using ¼in (6mm) seam allowance

leave open

FIG 2

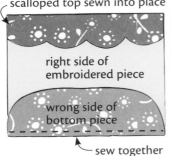

scalloped top sewn into place

right side of embroidered piece

wrong side of bottom piece

sew together

bag front

making the handles

10 From print fabric cut four 1¾ x 13in (4.5 x 33cm) strips for handles. From iron-on wadding cut two strips 1¾ x 13in (4.5 x 33cm). For longer handles simply increase the length measurement. Following the manufacturer's instructions, fuse the iron-on wadding to the wrong sides of two of the handle strips.

11 Take one of the bag handle strips with wadding and place it right sides together with a plain strip. Machine stitch together down both long sides using a ¼in (6mm) seam, leaving the ends open. Repeat this for other handle. Turn the handles through to the right side and press flat. Sew a row of machine stitching ¼in (6mm) in from each edge and then a row in the centre – these will make the handle firmer. Repeat for other handle.

assembling the bag

12 Pin the bag handles into position (see Fig 4). Take the bag lining and the bag outer, and with right sides together and lining up the seams around the top edge, pin together. Make sure that the bag handles are inside! Once you have everything in place use a ¼in (6mm) seam machine stitch around the top edge of the bag.

FIG 4

13 Turn the bag through to the right side through the opening left earlier in the side seam of the lining. Stitch the opening in the lining closed. Gently press around the top edge of the bag, making sure that the lining is not peeking over the edge and showing on the front of the bag. For a professional look, machine stitch close to the top edge of the bag. All finished – enjoy your gorgeous bag.

needle case

This handy needle case is a perfect companion to the bag and scissor keeper. It has two pockets inside, with room for various stitching accessories, such as thimbles, packets of needles and reels of threads. A wool patch keeps your pins and needles safe. As an extra finishing touch you could customize the case with your name on an appliquéd patch. Finished size (closed) 7 x 5¼in (18 x 13.5cm) approximately.

You will need...

- 6½ x 10½in (16.5 x 26.7cm) of green wool for case outer

- 6½ x 10½in (16.5 x 26.7cm) each of two coordinating prints

- 6 x 9in (15 x 23cm) of cream-on-cream print for stitchery

- 2½ x 3½in (6.3 x 9cm) of red wool for needle holder inside case

- 6 x 9in (15 x 23cm) iron-on stabilizer (optional)

- 2in (5cm) strip x width of fabric for binding

- DMC stranded cotton:
  country red (221)
  dirty green (3011)
  lime green (3819)
  black (310)

- One dog-shaped button (see Suppliers)

- Template plastic

- Fine-tipped fabric marking pen in brown

working the stitchery

1 Using the templates on page 114, transfer the two stitchery designs on to the right side of the cream-on-cream print, leaving 2in (5cm) between designs to cut them apart later. Iron on the fusible stabilizer now, if using. Follow the instructions on page 12 for working the embroidery on the outside and inside of the case.

making the needle case

2 From one of the coordinating prints cut a piece 6½ x 10½in (16.5 x 26.7cm) for the needle case lining. Choose another coordinating print and cut a piece 5½ x 10½in (14 x 26.7cm) for the inner pocket.

3 Using the template on page 114 make a pattern from template plastic for the arch shape, adding a ¼in (6mm) seam allowance. With the stitchery face up, centre the arch template over the stitchery. With a fabric marking pen or 2B pencil carefully draw around the template and cut out ¼in (6mm) beyond the line (see Fig 1). Turn under the ¼in (6mm) seam all round the arch shape, tack (baste) it in place and press.

FIG 1

Template on wrong side of fabric

Turn under ¼in (6mm) seam allowance

4 Take the 6½ x 10½in (16.5 x 26.7cm) wool case outer and press in half to become 6½ x 5¼in (16.5 x 13.3cm). Pin the arched stitchery design on the front of the case. Stitch down using a blind hem stitch. Remove tacking (basting) stitches (Fig 2).

FIG 2

making the inner pocket

5 Take the 5½ x 10½in (14 x 26.7cm) pocket piece and fold in half lengthwise. Press the pocket in half widthwise (Fig 3) and then fold the right-hand half into two (there will be a ¼in (6mm) seam at each end). Press lightly to crease the halves.

FIG 3

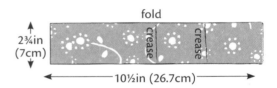

5½in (14cm) — pocket piece — 10½in (26.7cm)

fold — 2¾in (7cm) — crease — crease — 10½in (26.7cm)

6 Trim the inner pocket stitchery down to 2½in x 4¾in (6.3cm x 12cm). Tacking the seam under as you go, turn under about ¼in (6mm) and press. Position the stitchery using the picture as a guide, stitch in place using a blind hem stitch and remove the tacking stitches.

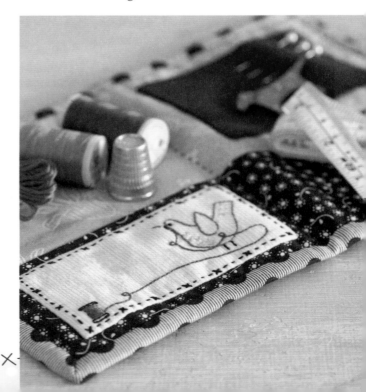

making the needle case inner

7 Take the 6½ x 10½in (16.5 x 26.7cm) lining cut previously and position the pocket, pinning it in place (Fig 4).

FIG 4

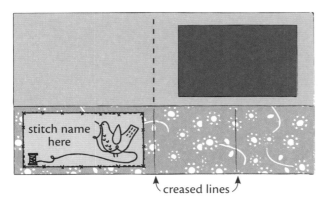

stitch name here

‹ creased lines ›

8 Using two strands of DMC stranded cotton 221 (country red) and backstitch, stitch on the creased lines you made previously, making sure you stitch through the layers of the pocket and the needle case lining.

9 Position the red wool for the needle holder and pin in place (Fig 5). Using two strands of black stranded cotton, blanket stitch around the edges to hold it in place. Gently press your work. Using matching sewing thread, stitch the dog button into position.

FIG 5

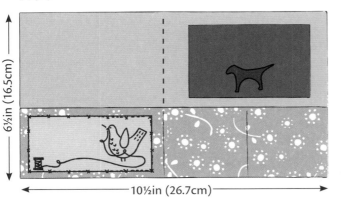

6½in (16.5cm)

10½in (26.7cm)

finishing the needle case

10 Take the embroidered needle case outer and the embroidered inner, place them wrong sides together and pin. Measure all the way around the outer edge, add about 4in (10cm) and note this measurement – it should be about 38in (96.5cm).

11 For the binding cut a strip on the straight grain from one of your coordinating prints 1⅜in (3.5cm) wide x the necessary length (the measurement you noted in step 10). Press in ¼in (6mm) down the length of the binding. With the needle case front facing you, place the unpressed edge of the binding on the edge of case, right sides together (Fig 6). Pin and machine stitch the binding into place all round using a ¼in (6mm) seam (see page 109 for more instructions on binding).

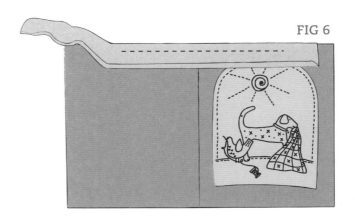

FIG 6

12 Turn the pressed edge of the binding to the inside of the needle case and slip stitch into place, with the stitches just covering the line of machine stitching. Your needle case is now finished, ready for its accessories.

scissor keeper

This handy little scissor keeper is perfect to keep your sharp embroidery scissors safe. It is made of card covered with fabric, so it remains rigid. A twisted cord and little tassel made from black embroidery thread keeps your scissors within easy reach.
Finished size (excluding cord) 4 x 2½in (10 x 6.5cm) approximately.

You will need...

- 8in (20.3cm) square of print fabric for back

- 8in (20.3cm) square of cream-on-cream print for stitchery

- 8in (20.3cm) square of iron-on stabilizer (optional)

- DMC stranded cotton:
  country red (221)
  dirty green (3011)
  lime green (3819)
  black (310)

- Fast-tack glue that dries clear

- Thin wadding (batting) or pellon

- Thin card

- Template plastic

- Fine-tipped fabric marking pen in brown

working the stitchery

1 Using the templates on page 113, transfer the two stitchery designs for the scissor keeper on to the right side of the cream-on-cream print, leaving 2in (5cm) between designs to cut them apart later. Iron on the fusible stabilizer now, if using. Follow the instructions on page 12 for working the embroidery.

TIP
I like to recycle materials when I can so a cereal packet is useful to cut up and use for the card inside the scissor keeper.

making the keeper

2 Using the templates on page 113 make templates from template plastic for the two scissor holder shapes. Place the templates on to the wrong side of your stitchery and making sure the stitchery is centred, draw around the template with a pencil. Cut out these shapes about ⅜in (1cm) beyond the drawn line to allow for a seam. Use the same templates to mark the shapes on your print backing fabric, cutting out approximately ⅜in (1cm) beyond the drawn line to allow for a seam.

> **TIP**
> To ensure that stitchery is centred on the card, hold it up to a light with the card shape behind – you will easily see if you have it in the right place.

3 Use the templates to mark the shapes on thin wadding (batting) but this time no seam allowance is needed, so cut out the shapes exactly on the line. Use the templates to mark the shapes on thick card, cutting out the shapes exactly on the line. Cut two card pieces for each shape.

4 Take one card back piece and one card front piece and glue thin wadding on to one side of each of them (Fig 1).

FIG 1

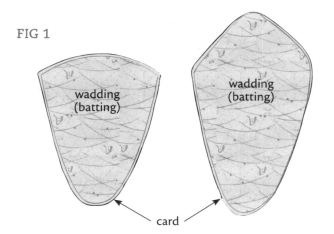

wadding (batting)

wadding (batting)

card

5 Place the stitchery for the front of the scissor keeper wrong side up and place the appropriate card shape on top, wadding side up. Carefully put glue around the edge of the card and then bring the ¼in (6mm) seam allowance over the edge on to the glue (Fig 2). Hold in place while the glue is drying. Do the same for the other piece of stitchery and the back piece of card. Repeat this process with the other pieces of card and the backing fabric pieces (Fig 3). Place these four pieces aside for the moment.

FIG 2

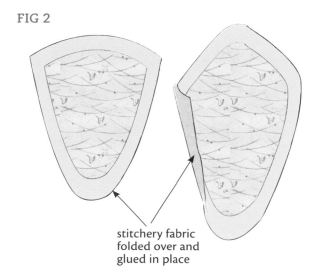

stitchery fabric folded over and glued in place

FIG 3

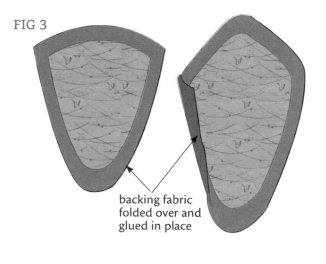

backing fabric folded over and glued in place

X—X—X—X—X—X—X—X—X—X—X—X—X—X—

making the tassel and cord

6 To make the tassel, cut a piece of card 1¼in (3.2cm) wide. Cut black stranded cotton about 30in (76cm) long and wrap it around the card about twenty times. Start counting wraps from the bottom of the card. When you have the desired size of tassel, slide it off the card.

7 To make the cord, take two lengths of black stranded cotton about 48in (120cm) long. Anchor one end of the two threads under something heavy or ask a friend to hold one end firmly. Twist the threads in a clockwise direction until the cord wants to double back on itself, but don't let it yet! Thread the twisted cord through the top loops of the tassel, centre the tassel on the cord and now let the cord double back on itself. Hold on to the ends while it twists and then tie a small knot at the end to secure it. Cut through the bottom loops of the tassel. Take a short length of thread and wrap it around the tassel about ¼in (6mm) from the top loop. Secure with a knot and put the thread ends out of sight.

assembling the scissor keeper

8 Take your four pieces of covered card and check that the glue has dried. Place the front pieces of the scissor holder, wrong sides together, and glue them together. Whilst the glue is drying you could use washing pegs or bulldog clips to hold the layers together to ensure they bond well. Repeat the process with the two back pieces but first place the end of the twisted cord in the centre top between the two back pieces. You now have a back and a front for your scissor holder.

9 Using two strands of black stranded cotton and herringbone stitch, join the front and back pieces together, stitching the seam of the top front edge of the scissor holder (Fig 4). Still using herringbone stitch, join the front to the back, stitching all around the edge. Your scissor holder is now finished.

FIG 4

kitty cat in the garden

A beautiful quilt in warm late summer colours is perfect as a blanket on the grass for an impromptu picnic or thrown over a bench as you enjoy the garden. The quilt is adorned with little stitched panels, featuring a contented cat, a little blue bird and some yoyo flowers, appliquéd in place and with a rustic frayed edge. The quilt blocks are simple squares and rectangles so it is easy to piece together. With its cosy colours and charming stitcheries, the quilt would be a most welcoming sight in a guest bedroom.

A pretty, fabric-covered journal matches the quilt and uses one of the embroidered panels, plus some jumbo ric-rac braid to decorate the front of the journal. It would be the perfect gift for a friend or to take to quilt shows to note down all those gorgeous fabrics you like.

bed quilt

This lovely quilt would look just as beautiful in a bedroom as in a garden and its mellow colours would suit many decors. The little stitched and appliquéd panels are easy to do and give a charming, tactile quality to the quilt, although you could omit them if preferred. Finished size 55 x 55in (140 x 140cm) approximately.

You will need...

- 8in (20cm) of cream-on-cream print across the fabric width for stitchery background

- ¼yd (0.25m) each of twelve coordinating prints

- 1yd (1m) of blue print for border

- 12in (30cm) of red print for backing the stitcheries and the inner binding

- Blue wool for appliqué birds

- Scraps of fabric 2½in (6.3cm) wide, totalling about 6½yd (6m) for binding

- DMC stranded cotton: black (310), blue (926), green (3012), dark brown (3781), soft red (3830) and light brown (3862)

- 6in (15cm) iron-on stabilizer for stitchery, across the width (optional)

- Fine-tipped fabric marking pen in brown

- Template plastic

- Wadding (batting) 63in (160cm) square

- Backing fabric 63in (160cm) square

making the yoyos

1 Make a template from template plastic using the yoyo pattern on page 115. From assorted print fabrics make eighteen yoyos following the instructions on page 107. Place the yoyos aside for later use.

working the stitchery

2 Using the templates on page 115, transfer the stitchery designs on to the right side of the cream-on-cream print (see page 104 for transferring designs), leaving about 2in (5cm) between designs to cut them apart later. Iron on the fusible stabilizer now, if using. You need three cat stitcheries, three yoyo flower stitcheries and three 'meow' stitcheries. Follow the instructions overleaf for stitching the designs. The bird appliqués are done later.

> **TIP**
> If you like working with an embroidery hoop remember to allow a little more fabric so it can be mounted in the hoop.

3 Once all the stitching has been completed, press the pieces. Trim each of the cat pieces to 4½in x 6in (11.4cm x 15.2cm). Trim the yoyo flower pieces to 3¾in x 4½in (9.5cm x 11.4cm) and the 'meow' pieces to 2¼in x 3¾in (5.7cm x 9.5cm).

4 On all of the pieces, turn approximately ¼in (6mm) to the back, tack (baste) in place and press. Using the picture as a guide position the yoyos and stitch in place. Place the stitcheries in a safe place for later.

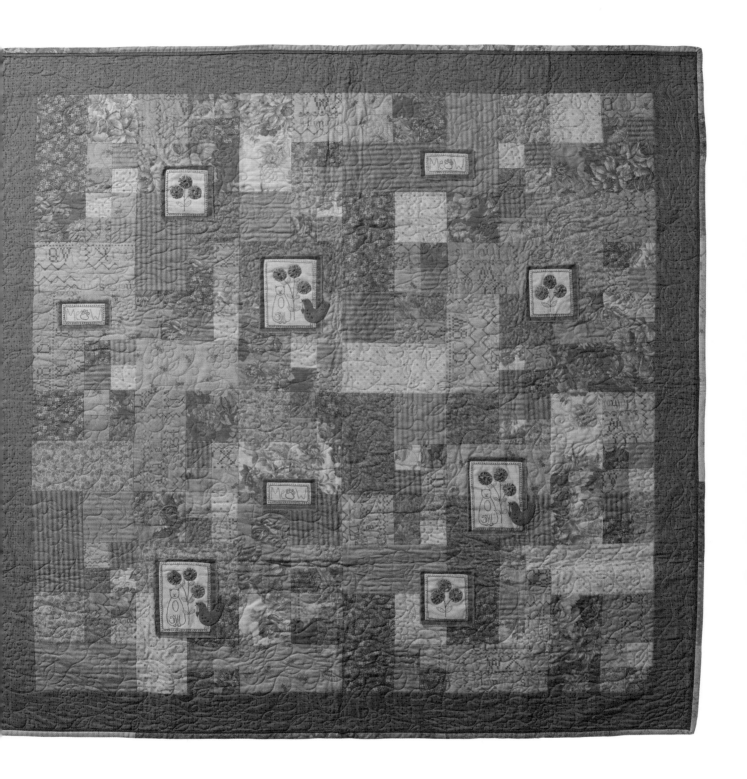

working the embroidery

Once the designs are transferred on to your fabrics you can work the stitches. I used DMC stranded cotton, using two strands of stranded cotton (unless otherwise stated). The colours used on the bed quilt were black (310), blue (926), green (3012), dark brown (3781), soft red (3830) and light brown (3862). The stitches used are as follows, with abbreviations in brackets: backstitch (BS), cross stitch (CS), French knots (FK), running stitch (RS) and satin stitch (SS). See page 110 for how to work all the stitches.

key for threads and stitches

 DMC 310 (black)
Cat's eyes and mouth (BS, one strand)
String holding the heart (BS)
Bird's eye (FK)
Markings on bird's tail (RS)
Markings on bird's chest (BS)

 DMC 926 (blue)
X's in outer border of cat block (CS)

 DMC 3012 (green)
Leaves (BS)
X's in outer border of meow and yoyo blocks (CS)

 DMC 3781 (dark brown)
Flower stems on cat and yoyo block (BS)
Paw print on meow block (BS)

 DMC 3830 (soft red)
Hanging heart on cat block (SS)
Letters on meow block (BS)

 DMC 3862 (light brown)
Cat (BS)
Bird's beak (SS)

making the quilt blocks

5 From each of the twelve fabrics cut twelve 2½in (6.3cm) squares, three 4½in (11.4cm) squares and three 4½ x 8½in (11.4 x 21.6cm) rectangles (see Fig 1 below as a guide for cutting).

FIG 1

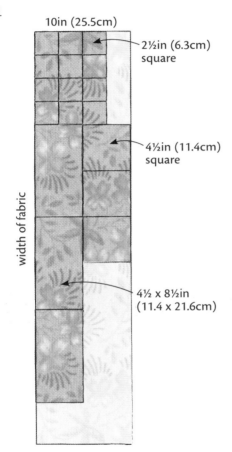

10in (25.5cm)

2½in (6.3cm) square

4½in (11.4cm) square

width of fabric

4½ x 8½in (11.4 x 21.6cm)

TIP
For a lovely scrappy look to your quilt use fabrics from your stash, and challenge yourself to only use each fabric a couple of times in the quilt.

6 Following Fig 2 and using a ¼in (6mm) seam allowance join the square and rectangular pieces to make a block, with a finished size of 8½in (21.6cm) square. Press the seams as you piece the block. Make thirty-six of these blocks in total.

FIG 2

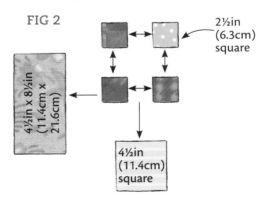

2½in (6.3cm) square

4½in x 8½in (11.4cm x 21.6cm)

4½in (11.4cm) square

completed block

7 Using ¼in (6mm) seams join the blocks in six rows each with six blocks (Fig 3a). You could rotate some of the blocks to give a random look to the quilt. Join the six rows together to form the quilt top (Fig 3b). Press the work.

FIG 3

A

B

row 1

row 2

row 3

row 4

row 5

row 6

adding the borders

8 You may wish to measure your quilt top before cutting fabric for the borders, in case your measurements differ from mine. From blue border fabric cut two pieces for the top and bottom border, each 4 x 48½in (10.2 x 123.2cm) (or to your quilt measurements) and then cut two pieces 4 x 55½in (10.2 x 141cm) for the side borders (or to your measurements).

9 Using a ¼in (6mm) seam join the top and bottom borders to the centre panel and press. Join the side borders in the same way and press. See page 107 for more on adding borders.

decorating the quilt

10 Use the bird template on page 115 to cut three birds from wool – you do not need to turn the edges under on the wool as it will not fray.

11 From the red print cut three pieces 4¼ x 4½in (11.4 x 11.4cm), three pieces 4⅞ x 6¼in (12.4 x 15.9cm) and three pieces 2¼ x 3¾in (5.7 x 9.5cm). On all pieces fray the edges for about ¼in (6mm).

12 Take the stitcheries and put them in place on the quilt top, using the picture on page 29 as a guide for positioning. Place one of the frayed pieces under each stitchery – this will stick out beyond the stitchery, framing it. Pin together through all the layers and stitch on to the quilt top using a blind hem stitch.

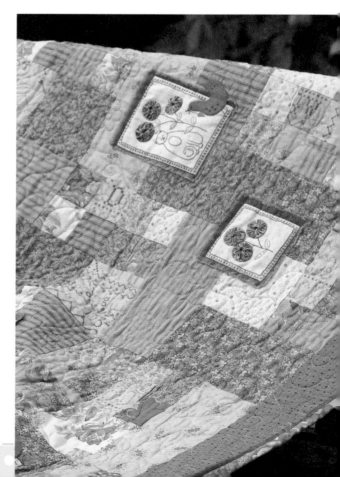

13 Using the pictures as a guide, position the wool birds and blanket stitch them in place using two strands of DMC 926 (blue). If you haven't already worked the embroidery stitches on the bird see key on page 30 for details.

quilting

14 I had my quilt professionally machine quilted with an all-over pattern – see page 108 for advice.

adding the bindings

15 To make the inner binding, from red print cut six 1in (2.5cm) wide strips, join them together and press in half lengthwise. With the right side of quilt facing up, and doing one side at a time, align the raw edge of the inner binding with the raw edge of the quilt and stitch in place with a scant ¼in (6mm) seam allowance. Repeat for the other three sides. For the outer binding, join together all your 2½in (6.3cm) wide fabric scraps into one long length and follow the directions on page 109.

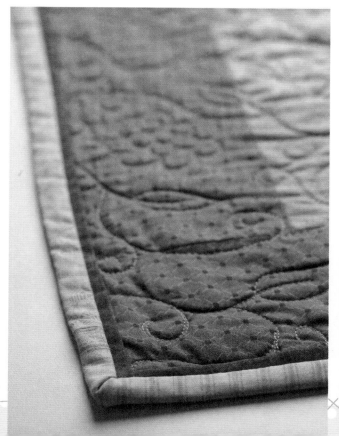

journal

A fabric-covered journal decorated with some sweet stitchery is perfect for a relaxing afternoon in the garden – perhaps taking notes on what seeds to grow next year or using the journal as a diary to record thoughts and memories. Little yoyos bring a three-dimensional touch to the embroidery and appliqué. Fabrics listed below are across the width of the fabric unless otherwise stated.

Finished size 8¼in x 6¼in (21cm x 16cm).

You Will Need

- 30cm (12in) blue floral fabric for journal cover

- 30cm (12in) print fabric for journal lining

- 20cm (8in) square of cream-on-cream print for stitchery

- Scraps of three assorted prints for yoyos

- Scrap of wool for bird

- 1m (1yd) of wide ric-rac braid

- 30cm (12in) of lightweight iron-on wadding (batting) or pellon

- 20cm (8in) square of iron-on stabilizer (optional)

- One journal – mine was 8¼in x 6¼in (21cm x 16cm)

- DMC stranded cotton: black (310), blue (926), green (3012), dark brown (3781), soft red (3830) and light brown (3862)

- Fine-tipped fabric marking pen in brown

- Template plastic

making the yoyos

1 Create a yoyo template from template plastic and the pattern on page 115. Make three yoyos from assorted fabrics following the directions on page 107. Place the completed yoyos to one side for the moment.

working the stitchery

2 Using the template on page 115, transfer the stitchery design for the journal on to the right side of the cream-on-cream print (see page 104 for transferring designs). Iron on the fusible stabilizer now, if using. Follow the instructions overleaf for stitching the designs. The bird appliqué is done later.

3 Once all the stitching has been completed, stitch the yoyos made earlier into place, using the picture as a guide. Trim the stitchery for the front of the journal to 4½ x 6in (11.4 x 15.2cm). Turn about ¼in (6mm) of the stitchery to the back, tack (baste) in place and press.

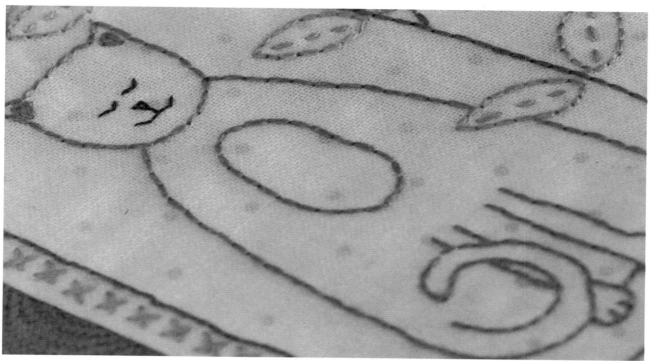

working the embroidery

Once the designs are transferred on to your fabrics you can work the stitches. I used DMC stranded cotton, using two strands of stranded cotton (unless otherwise stated). The colours used on the journal were black (310), blue (926), dark brown (3781), soft red (3830) and light brown (3862). The stitches used were (abbreviations in brackets): backstitch (BS), cross stitch (CS), French knots (FK), running stitch (RS) and satin stitch (SS). See page 110 for how to work the stitches.

key for threads and stitches

DMC 310 (black)
Cat's eyes and mouth (BS, one strand)
String holding the heart (BS)
Bird's eye (FK)
Markings on bird's tail (RS)
Markings on bird's chest (BS)

DMC 926 (blue)
X's in outer border (CS)

DMC 3781 (dark brown)
Flower stems (BS)
Line of outer border (BS)

DMC 3830 (soft red)
Hanging heart (SS)

DMC 3862 (light brown)
Cat (BS)
Bird's beak (SS)
Bird's legs (BS)

making the journal cover

4 To cover a journal with a front measuring 8¼ x 6¼in (21 x 16cm), cut one piece of blue floral fabric 9 x 18½in (23 x 47cm). Cut the same size from the iron-on wadding (batting) and from lining fabric. Following the manufacturer's instructions bond the iron-on wadding to the wrong side of the blue floral fabric.

5 To make cover, place the journal outer and lining fabric right sides together and stitch around the edge using ¼in (6mm) seam allowance. Leave a small opening about 3in (7.6cm) wide at the bottom (Fig 1). Clip corners and turn right side out.

FIG 1

+ - - leave open here - - +

6 Press lightly, making sure that none of the lining fabric can be seen from the front. Lay the cover flat, lining side up, centre the journal on the cover and measure the turn-back required, allowing for the spine of the book. Fold in the turn-back and hand stitch in place (Fig 2).

FIG 2

hand stitch fold-back into place

7 Work out where the centre of the front cover is and position the stitchery. Lay the ric-rac braid just under the stitchery (Fig 3) and when happy with the position, pin in place and stitch.

FIG 3

8 Use the bird appliqué template on page 115 to cut the shape from your wool. Position the bird on the embroidery and hold it in place with blanket stitch – I used two strands of stranded cotton to match the wool. Stitch the markings on the bird's chest and tail as described opposite.

woof! woof!

This quilt was inspired by Hugo, a loving puppy who came into our lives at twelve weeks old. He arrived with a special jacket showing he was in training for Seeing Eye Dogs Australia. For a year I took Hugo everywhere I went and with his special jacket he created a lot of interest. Unfortunately Hugo did not pass his Seeing Eye Dog final tests and although we were initially disappointed it meant we could keep him as our pet. Some of the dogs on this quilt are wearing service jackets as a tribute to dogs worldwide that help others, and to celebrate the dedication of puppy trainers. Why not think about sponsoring a puppy or becoming a puppy carer?

This quilt with its repeated dog and bird block can be made in any size. Some of the blocks are flipped to give a more random look to the quilt. A friend of mine machine quilted it to great effect and I particularly love how she has stitched a fence outline behind the dogs.

If you want to practise the techniques used in the quilt on a smaller project first then make the wonderful cushion on page 46. It would look great in any setting.

best friend quilt 🖤

The fabrics chosen for this wonderful folk art-style quilt are rich reds, blues, greens and tans, which are set off nicely against warm creams. Apart from the dog and bird blocks there are also Friendship Star blocks and tree blocks, interspersed with hearts and paw prints. The blocks can be mixed and matched to create a great looking quilt which is unique to you. The appliqué shapes are easy to create and use a needle-turn technique.
Finished size: 64 x 84in (162 x 213cm) approximately.

You will need...

- 0.5m (½yd), each of six assorted cream-on-cream prints

- 10in (25cm) each of two brown prints (width of fabric)

- A fat quarter of dark brown print

- Five different fat quarters each of green fabrics, blue fabrics and red fabrics

- ¾yd (0.75m) of dark green fabric for inner border

- DMC stranded embroidery cotton: black (310), country red (221) and dark brown (838)

- Template plastic

- Twelve tiny buttons for dogs' eyes (optional)

- 70 x 90in (178 x 228cm) of wadding (batting)

- 70 x 90in (178 x 228cm) of backing fabric

- 22in (56cm) of fabric for binding (width of fabric)

making the friendship star blocks

1 From cream-on-cream fabric cut two 2⅞in (7.3cm) squares and four 2½in (6.3cm) squares. From a green, blue or red print cut two 2⅞in (7.3cm) squares and one 2½in (6.3cm) square.

2 On the wrong side of the fabric and using a 2B pencil or fabric marking pen draw a line diagonally from corner to corner on both the 2⅞in (7.3cm) cream squares (see Fig 1). Place a square with a drawn line on it right sides together with a print square of the same size. Pin together if you feel you need to. Stitch together with a ¼in (6mm) seam either side of the drawn line. Carefully cut across the drawn line and press open.

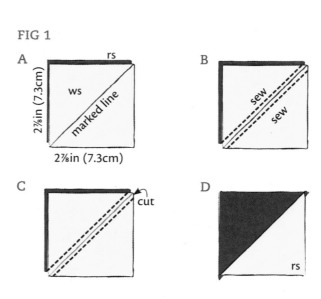

FIG 1

3 Following the layout shown in Fig 2 place the pieces of the star on your work surface and stitch together using a ¼in (6mm) seam allowance. Make twenty-four star blocks in total.

FIG 2

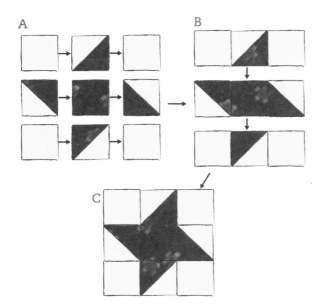

making the dog and bird blocks

4 From assorted background fabrics cut twelve rectangles each 9½ x 12½in (24.1 x 31.7cm). Make templates from template plastic for the dog, his ear, collar, jacket and the bird from the templates on page 116. (See page 104 for using templates.) I have applied my shapes using needle-turn appliqué (see page 105 for instructions).

> **TIP**
> I arranged the dog and bird blocks facing different ways to add interest to the quilt. If you want to do this then you will need to turn the template over to reverse the shapes.

5 Using an appropriate marking pen, trace around your plastic templates on the wrong side of your chosen fabrics. Cut out the shapes but make sure to allow for a ¼in (6mm) seam allowance all round. See Tip below on reversing blocks.

6 For each fabric shape fold the raw edge to the wrong side of fabric using the drawn line as a guide and tack (baste) in place (Fig 3). Clip the seam allowance to ensure a smooth curve when turning under edges on concave curves (inward ones). Press the folds.

FIG 3

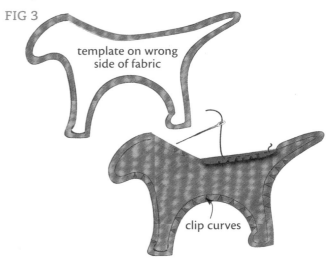

template on wrong side of fabric

clip curves

7 Place the shapes on to the right side of a background fabric (Fig 4). Once happy with the position, pin in place and apply the shapes with an invisible stitch, such as blind hem. Make twelve dog and bird blocks in total.

making the tree blocks

8 From assorted background fabrics cut twelve pieces each 18½ x 6½in (47 x 16.5cm). Make templates from template plastic for the tree and small heart as you did for the dog. You have already made the bird template. Trace round the templates on the wrong side of your fabrics. Cut out, allowing for a ¼in (6mm) seam allowance all round.

9 Prepare the appliqués as you did before. Position them on your background rectangles and stitch in place. Make twelve tree blocks in total.

making the heart and paw blocks

10 From assorted fabrics cut a total of forty-eight 3½in (8.9cm) squares. Take four squares (each one a different fabric) and with ¼in (6mm) seam allowances join them together to form a strip 3½ x 12½in (8.9 x 31.7cm) – see Fig 4. Make twelve of these strips.

FIG 4

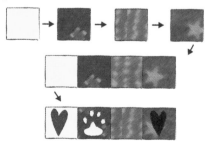

11 Make templates from template plastic for the large heart and paw print, as before. Prepare the appliqués as in step 6. Position the shapes on your background strips and stitch in place. I have kept the shapes in the same position on all of the strips but you could vary yours.

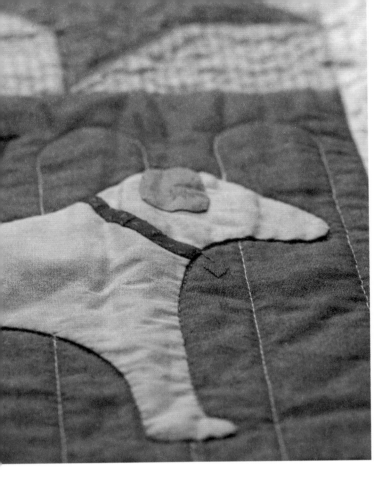

adding the stitchery

12 Now you have made all the blocks it's time to add the decorative stitching. With a suitable fabric marking pen and using the templates as a guide to placement, carefully mark the birds' legs and beaks, the dogs' name tags, the tree branches and the string holding the heart in the trees. Sew on buttons for the dogs' eyes if you wish (see Tip below). Embroider the finer details using two strands of embroidery thread as follows.

- Backstitch the birds' legs in brown.
- Satin stitch the birds' beaks in brown.
- Satin stitch the dogs' heart name tags in red.
- Backstitch the heart string and bow in black.
- Chain stitch the tree branches in dark brown.

> **Tip**
> The buttons for the dogs' eyes are optional as you may want to give the quilt to a young child and prefer not to use buttons. If you do, sew them on securely with strong thread.

joining the blocks

13 You can now decide on the block arrangement. I varied the position of the stars and the heart and paw blocks. For the first and third row I put the tree on the right side of the dog and for the second and fourth rows I put the tree on the left side of the dog. Using ¼in (6mm) seam allowances join two rows of three blocks with the tree on the right (Fig 5) and two rows of three blocks with the tree on the left. Then, alternating the two rows, join them together to form four rows of three. Press well.

FIG 5

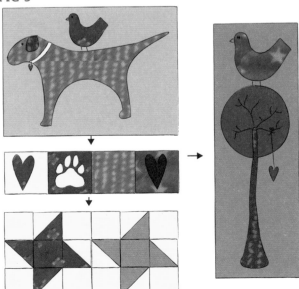

making the borders

14 To make the inner border, from the border fabric cut three 2½in (6.3cm) strips across the fabric width and using a ¼in (6mm) seam allowance join them to make two 2½ x 54½in (6.3 x 138.4cm) strips. These strips are for the top and bottom borders. Cut four 1½in (3.8cm) strips and join them to make two 1½ x 76½in (3.8 x 194.3cm) strips. These strips are for the side borders. Sew these strips to the centre of the quilt, attaching the top and bottom borders first.

15 To make the outer border, take the 4½in (11.4cm) squares that were cut from the appliqué fabrics earlier and, using a ¼in (6mm) seam allowance, join to form two rows of fourteen and two rows of twenty-one. These will be the top and bottom borders and side borders respectively. Sew on the top and bottom borders to the centre panel first, and then sew on the two side borders.

FIG 6

quilt centre panel

quilting and finishing

16 Make a quilt sandwich from the quilt top, wadding (batting) and backing, as described on page 108 and quilt your work. Bind the quilt to finish – see page 109 for instructions. My quilt was machine quilted but you could hand quilt your own patterns if you prefer. The machine quilting was as follows.

- Echo quilting around all the appliqué shapes.
- Picket fence pattern quilted in the background of all the dog and bird blocks.
- Machine quilting in a paw pattern in the plain blocks in the paw and heart strips.
- Free-motion star and heart pattern in the background of the tree and star blocks and in the inner border.
- Free machine-quilted paw print pattern in the outer border.

good boy cushion

What dog-adoring person would not love to have this very special cushion? It's also the perfect project to practise the techniques for the Best Friend Quilt.
Finished size 18½ x 18½in (47 x 47cm).

making the friendship star blocks

1 From cream-on-cream fabric cut two 2⅞in (7.3cm) squares and four 2½in (6.3cm) squares. From print fabric cut two 2⅞in (7.3cm) squares and one 2½in (6.3cm) square.

2 On the wrong side of the fabric and with a 2B pencil or fabric marking pen draw a line diagonally from corner to corner on both the 2⅞in (7.3cm) cream squares (Fig 1). Place a square with a drawn line on it right sides together with a print square of the same size. Pin together if desired. Stitch together with a ¼in (6mm) seam either side of the drawn line. Cut along the drawn line and press open.

FIG 1

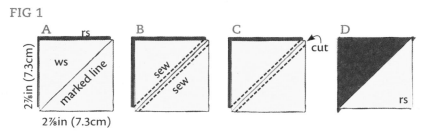

3 Following the layout in Fig 2 place the pieces of the star on your work surface and stitch together using a ¼in (6mm) seam allowance. Make two Friendship Star blocks.

FIG 2

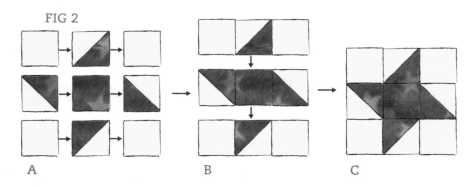

making the dog and bird block

4 From background fabric cut one rectangle 9½ x 12½in (24.1 x 31.7cm). Make templates from template plastic for the dog, his ear, his collar and the bird from the templates on page 116. (See page 104 for using templates.) I have applied my shapes using traditional needle-turn appliqué (see page 105 for details).

5 Using an appropriate marking pen, trace around your plastic templates on wrong side of your chosen fabrics. Cut out the shapes but make sure to allow for a ¼in (6mm) seam allowance all round.

6 For each fabric shape fold the raw edge to the wrong side of the fabric using the drawn line as a guide and tack (baste) in place (Fig 3). Remember to clip the seam allowance to ensure a smooth curve when turning under the edges on concave curves (inward ones). Press the folds.

FIG 3

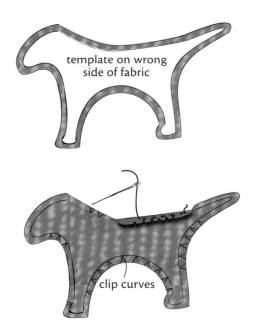

template on wrong side of fabric

clip curves

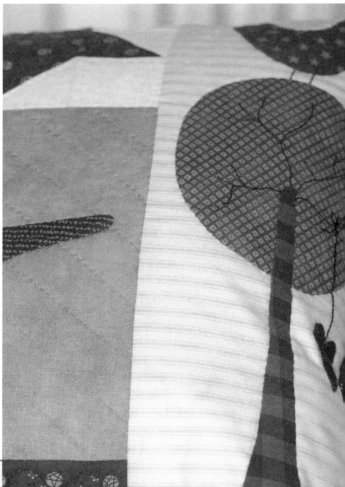

7 Place the shapes on to the right side of a background fabric (Fig 4). Pin in place and apply the shapes with an invisible stitch, such as a blind hem stitch.

making the tree block

8 From background fabric cut a 18½ x 6½in (47 x 16.5cm) rectangle. Make templates from template plastic for the tree and small heart as you did for the dog. You have already made the bird template. Trace around the templates on the wrong side of your chosen fabrics. Cut out, allowing for a ¼in (6mm) seam allowance all round.

9 Prepare the appliqué as you did before. Position on your background rectangle and stitch in place.

making the heart and paw block

10 From assorted fabrics cut four 3½in (8.9cm) squares and join together with ¼in (6mm) seams to form a strip 3½ x 12½in (8.9 x 31.7cm) – see Fig 4.

FIG 4

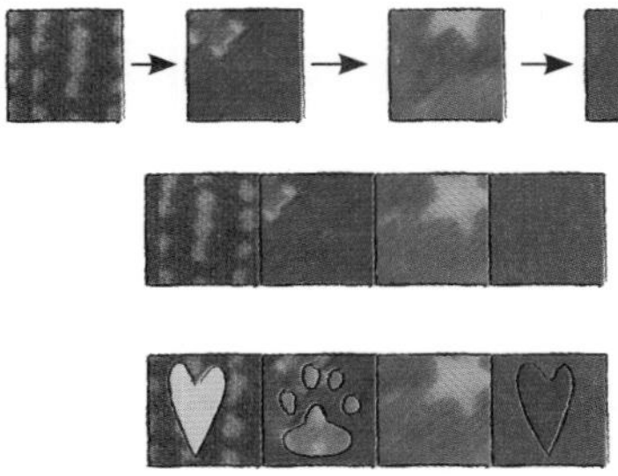

11 Make templates from template plastic for the large heart and the paw print and then prepare the appliqués as you did before. Position the shapes on your background strips and stitch in place.

adding the stitchery

12 With a suitable fabric marking pen and using the templates as a guide, carefully mark the birds' legs and beaks, the dog's name tag, the tree branches and the string holding the heart in the tree. Embroider the finer details using two strands of embroidery thread as follows.
- Backstitch the birds' legs and tails in brown.
- Satin stitch the birds' beaks in brown.
- Satin stitch the dog's heart name tag in red.
- Backstitch the heart string and bow in black.
- Chain stitch the tree branches in dark brown.

joining the blocks and quilting

13 Using ¼in (6mm) seam allowances join the blocks together in the arrangement shown in Fig 5. Press well.

FIG 5

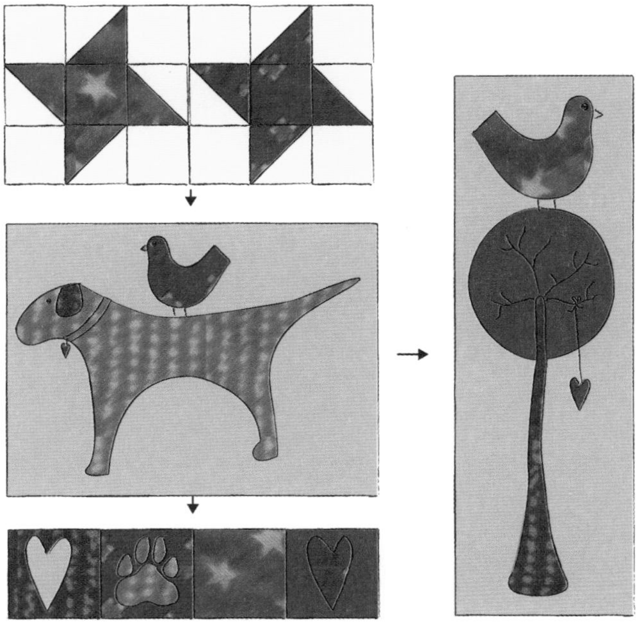

14 Make a sandwich from the cushion top, wadding (batting) and backing, as described on page 108 and quilt your work. I hand quilted the cushion as follows.
- Echo quilting to outline the star blocks.
- Grid quilting in the background of the dog and bird block.
- Heart outline quilted in heart and paw block.

making the cushion cover

15 Take the two 14½ x 18½in (36.8 x 47cm) pieces of cream backing fabric and press under ¼in (6mm) on one of the long sides of both pieces. Press under a further ¾in (2cm) and then machine stitch in place (see Fig 6).

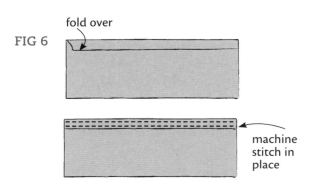

FIG 6

fold over

machine stitch in place

16 Place the two backing pieces together to make an 18½in (47cm) square, with the two pieces overlapping at the centre (Fig 7). Pin the Velcro fastenings in place on the back of the cushion and machine or hand stitch in place.

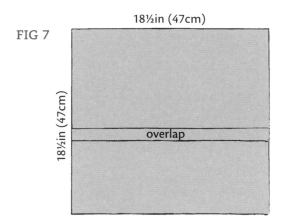

FIG 7

18½in (47cm)

18½in (47cm)

overlap

17 Stitch the 1in (2.5cm) diameter buttons over the Velcro using six strands of dark brown DMC stranded cotton. Start at the front of the button leave a tail of thread as you stitch the button in place. End the thread off by knotting the thread together at the front of the button. Stitch the three tiny buttons for eyes in place on the cushion front.

> **TIP**
> When sewing on the buttons, if you don't like the tails of thread left long simply sew the button on in the normal way.

18 Place the cushion back right side up and position the cushion front on top, right side down. Sew the two pieces together all round using a ¼in (6mm) seam. Press the seam. Bind the edge of the cushion all round – see page 109 for instructions. Insert the cushion pad into the cover.

i love my cat

This chapter gives you the chance to bring the cats in your life centre stage on a gorgeous wall hanging. I am a cat lover and cannot imagine our home without our three cats. Cats come in all shapes, sizes and colours and I had great fun representing my own pets in this quilt. It would be easy to change the colouring to suit your own cat family.

I combined several techniques in this quilt, including crazy patchwork, strip piecing and blanket stitch appliqué. I also had fun sponge painting the Siamese cat to get the realistic look I wanted. For the fabrics I chose denim blues and tans as I really like how these colours work together and think they give a lively look to the quilt.

If you want a really quick project you could create some pincushions for friends and family. A circular shape with some easy appliqué creates a sweet curled-up cat everyone will love – see page 62.

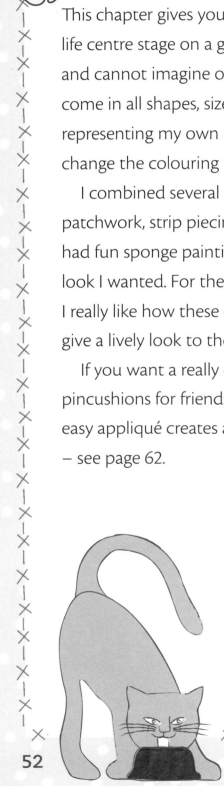

cat lover wall quilt

Crazy Tom, Strippy Kitty and Siamese Girl are very much at home here on this delightful wall quilt. Have fun creating your cats' personalities by combining some crazy patchwork, some strip patchwork, blanket stitch appliqué and a little sponge painting.
Finished size 29 x 38in (73.5 x 96.5cm) approximately.

You will need...

- 12in (30cm) each of six coordinating fabrics, prints and plains (width of fabric)

- 10in (25cm) of a cream-on-cream print or tea-dyed calico

- 10in (25cm) of pale lightweight fabric, such as muslin

- Scrap of pale pink fabric

- ½yd (0.5m) fusible web

- Template plastic

- Small sea sponge and burnt umber acrylic paint

- DMC stranded cotton: dark brown (839), denim blue (3750), light fawn (841) and ecru

- 10in (25cm) of fabric for binding (width of fabric)

- Twelve assorted ⁵⁄₁₆in (16mm) diameter buttons and six ³⁄₁₆in (9mm) for cats' eyes

- Fine-tipped fabric pen

- 35 x 44in (89 x 112cm) of wadding (batting)

- 35 x 44in (89 x 112cm) of backing fabric

making the kitty likes milk block

1 Select two different fabrics and from one cut a piece 15½ x 10½in (39.4 x 26.7cm). From the other fabric cut a strip 15½ x 3½in (39.4 x 8.9cm). Sew the two pieces together along the long side and press the seam (Fig 1). This is the background block.

FIG 1

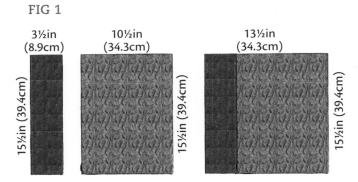

2 From template plastic make templates for the body, head, tail and bowl using the templates on page 117. (See page 104 for using templates.) Draw around the templates on to a pale, lightweight fabric, leaving a generous space between the body and tail so they can be cut out later, and space between the head and bowl too.

3 From each of the six coordinating fabrics cut a strip between ½–¾in (1.3–2cm). Starting at the cat's feet place a strip right side up, making sure it overlaps the drawn line, and pin in position (see Fig 2). Place the next strip right sides together on top of the first strip and machine stitch in place (just take a small seam allowance). Press open. Add strips in this way until the shape is covered.

FIG 2

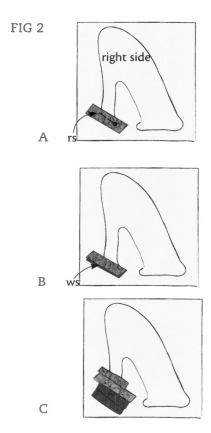

4 Using fusible web appliqué (see page 105) fuse the cat in the centre of the larger piece of fabric in the background block. Blanket stitch (see page 110) around the appliqués edges using two strands of light fawn for the body, denim blue for the head and ecru around the bowl and cat's tongue. Using the template as a guide, draw the features with a fine-tipped fabric pen. Using two strands of DMC stranded cotton and chain stitch sew the eyes, nose and mouth in denim blue. Backstitch the whiskers with dark brown.

making the crazy tom block

5 Select three fabrics. From one cut a piece 13½ x 3½in (34.3 x 8.9cm), from another cut a piece 6½ x 10½in (16.5 x 26.7cm) and from the third cut a piece 7½ x 10½in (19 x 26.7cm). Join the three pieces together (Fig 3). This is the background block.

FIG 3

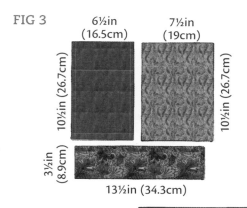

6 From template plastic make templates for the body, head and tail, using the templates on page 118. Draw around the templates on to the muslin leaving a generous space between the body, head and tail so they can be cut out later.

7 Choosing from the six coordinating fabrics, begin by cutting a five-sided scrap of fabric. Pin it in the centre of the foundation muslin, right side up (Fig 4). Take another scrap, place it right side down on one edge of the first scrap and machine or hand stitch it in place. Finger press open. Working clockwise continue adding scraps this way, pressing open each time, until the foundation is covered. Sew strips down the legs too. Press well.

FIG 4

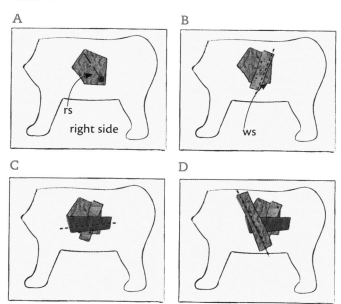

8 Using fusible web appliqué fuse Crazy Tom to the background block. Blanket stitch around the appliqué edges using two strands of denim blue for the body and face. Using the pattern as a guide, draw the face markings with a fine-tipped fabric pen. Using two strands of ecru stranded cotton and chain stitch sew the eyes, nose and mouth. Sew the whiskers in backstitch in ecru.

making the siamese girl block

9 Select two fabrics and from one cut a piece 8½ x 5½in (21.6 x 14cm) and from the second fabric cut a piece 8½ x 10½in (21.6 x 26.7cm). Join these two pieces together along the shortest sides (Fig 5). This is the background block.

FIG 5

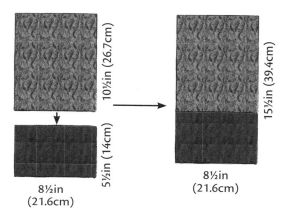

10 From template plastic make templates for the body and tail using the templates on page 117. Draw around the templates on to the cream-on-cream print or on tea-dyed calico (see Tip below), leaving a generous space between the body and the tail so they can be cut apart later.

> **TIP**
>
> To speckle tea-dye calico wet the fabric and squeeze out most of the water. Lay it flat and sprinkle generously with tea leaves. Long tea leaves create wonderful effects. Fold the tea-sprinkled fabric into a parcel, place on a plate, damp well and microwave on high for two minutes. It will be *hot* when you take it out, so take care. Open out and check the markings, repeating the cooking if necessary. Shake off the tea, rinse the fabric well and iron dry. If you want creases for effect, line dry for a short while and then press.

11 Wet a piece of sea sponge and squeeze out all the water. Load the sponge very *lightly* with burnt umber paint and lightly dab the paint on to parts of the cat to give a seal-point look –the forehead, nose, ears, lower front legs, paws and tail (see Fig 6). Practise on a spare piece of calico first. It is very important not to have the sponge too wet or to have too much paint. Leave to dry and then heat set the paint with a hot iron.

FIG 6

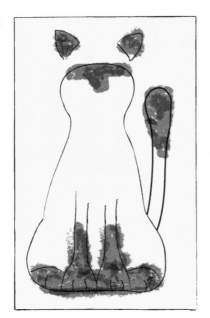

> **TIP**
> Even though the cat shape will be cut out, if you prefer you could create a negative template out of paper, so the paint can't go over the outlines on the fabric. Mark the body, tail and ears on the paper in exactly the same positions as on the fabric. Cut out the parts from the paper, leaving all the background intact. Place the marked fabric right side up on a work top, protected with paper. Place the paper template sheet on top, aligning the shapes with the marked shapes on the fabric. Sponge paint as in the step above.

12 Using fusible web appliqué fuse the Siamese cat to its background block. Blanket stitch around the edges of the appliqués using two strands of ecru for the paler parts of the body, changing to dark brown on the painted areas. Using the pattern as a guide, draw the markings for the cat's features and her legs and feet with a fine-tipped fabric pen. Using two strands of dark brown stranded cotton and chain stitch sew the eyes, nose, mouth, legs and feet. Sew the whiskers in backstitch in dark brown.

making the heart blocks

13 From assorted fabrics cut twelve pieces each 4½ x 5½in (11.4 x 14cm). Use the heart templates on page 117 to cut out the shapes in fabric.

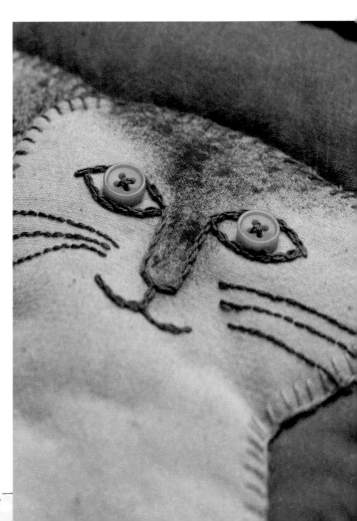

14 Using fusible web appliqué fuse a large heart on each of the background blocks. Fuse a smaller heart within the larger heart. Press well. Blanket stitch around the appliqués edges using two strands of denim blue, dark brown or ecru.

joining the blocks and making the borders

15 Join the blocks together with ¼in (6mm) seams as shown in Fig 7.

FIG 7

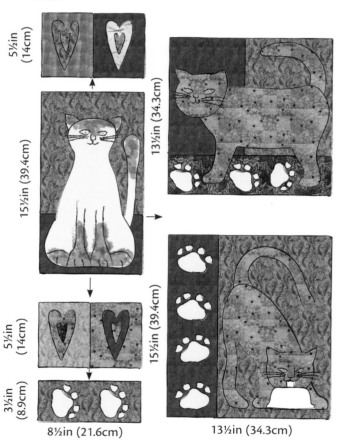

5½in (14cm)

15½in (39.4cm)

13½in (34.3cm)

5½in (14cm)

15½in (39.4cm)

3½in (8.9cm)

8½in (21.6cm)

13½in (34.3cm)

16 From assorted fabrics cut twenty-six 1½ x 5½in (3.8 x 14cm) strips for the top and bottom borders. Cut thirty-six 1½ x 4½in (3.8 x 11.4cm) strips for the side borders. Cut four pieces 5½ x 4½in (14 x 11.4cm) for the corner rectangles.

17 Take thirteen of the 1½ x 5½in (3.8 x 14cm) strips and join them together with two of the heart blocks to make the bottom border (see Fig 8).

Take another thirteen 1½ x 5½in (3.8 x 14cm) strips and join them together with two of the heart blocks to make the top border.

Take eighteen 1½ x 4½in (3.8 x 11.4cm) strips and join them together with two of the heart blocks and add a corner rectangle to each end for the left-hand side border.

Take another eighteen 1½ x 4½in (3.8 x 11.4cm) strips and join them together with two of the heart blocks and add a corner rectangle to each end for the right-hand side border. Sew these borders to the centre panel (Fig 9 opposite) and press well.

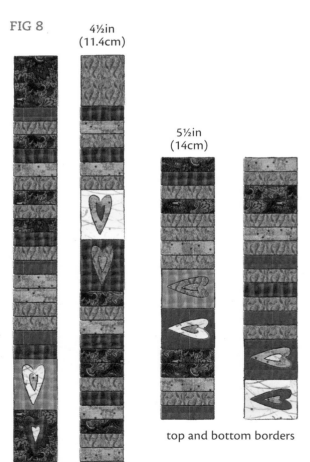

FIG 8

4½in (11.4cm)

5½in (14cm)

top and bottom borders

side borders

Tip
When measuring a quilt always measure across the centre to make sure that borders will be the correct size and to avoid creating wavy edges.

appliquéing the paw prints

18 Using the picture opposite as a guide for placement and fusible web appliqué, apply the paw prints. Use two strands of dark brown stranded cotton to blanket stitch the edges.

FIG 9

quilting and finishing

19 Make a quilt sandwich from the quilt top, wadding (batting) and backing, as described on page 108 and then quilt your work. I hand quilted as follows, but you could machine quilt if you prefer.
- Quilt in the ditch with a light-coloured thread between the cat blocks.
- Quilt around the cat shapes, around the appliquéd foot prints and the hearts.
- Quilt heart shapes in the striped border, marking the shape with the large heart template

20 Bind the quilt to finish (Fig 10 and see also page 109 for instructions). Sew the buttons in place through all thicknesses of the quilt, in the cats' eyes and in the centres of the appliquéd hearts in the outer border and in the small heart blocks within the quilt.

FIG 10

purrfect pincushion

Who could resist making one of these delightful sleeping cat pincushions for themselves? Once you discover how simple and quick they are you will be making one for all your stitching friends. There are two types of cat – one with appliquéd stripes and one with patches. The instructions and materials are to make one pincushion.
Finished size 4in (10.2cm) diameter approximately.

You will need...

- 8 x 14in (20 x 35.5cm) of main fabric

- 6in (15.2cm) square of contrast fabric

- 8 x 14in (20.3 x 35.5cm) lightweight iron-on wadding (batting) or pellon

- DMC stranded cottons to match/contrast with fabrics

- 8 x 14in (20.3 x 35.5cm) of fusible web

- Two buttons ½in (1.3cm) in diameter

- Doll maker's needle

- Template plastic

- Toy stuffing

- Fine-tipped fabric marking pen in brown

preparing the shapes

1 Using the templates on page 118 and template plastic, make templates for the body circle, the face and ears. (See page 104 for using templates.)

2 From your main fabric cut two from the body circle template, remembering to add a ¼in (6mm) seam allowance all round. From lightweight iron-on wadding cut two from the body circle template, adding ¼in (6mm) seam allowance all round. Following the manufacturer's instructions bond a piece of the wadding to the wrong side of each of the fabric circles. From main fabric and wadding cut one strip 1¾ x 13in (4.4 x 33cm), and bond these two together.

working the appliqué

3 Use the templates on page 118 for the stripes, paws and patches. You will need to *reverse* the templates (flip them over) if using fusible web appliqué. Using the fusible web method (see page 105) apply the stripes or patches to one of the body circles (Fig 1A). Apply the paws on the centre of the 1¾ x 13in (4.4 x 33cm) strip (Fig 1B). Work blanket stitch in two strands of matching stranded cotton around the appliqués. For the patches add long stitches in contrasting colour thread. Once stitching is complete gently press your work.

B

PAW APPLIQUES

preparing the face

4 From the main fabric and using the face template, place two pieces of fabric right sides together and trace around the template using a fabric marking pen. When cutting out add a ¼in (6mm) seam allowance all round. From lightweight iron-on wadding cut one from the face template, adding ¼in (6mm) seam allowance. Following the manufacturer's instructions bond a piece of the wadding to the wrong side of one piece of the face. Repeat this with the ear templates.

5 Placing the ear pieces right sides together, stitch around three sides of each ear, leaving the bottom open (Fig 2). Cut out, leaving a ⅛in (3mm) seam allowance all round. Clip off the seam allowance on the ear tip and turn through to the right side. Wriggle into shape and press gently.

FIG 2

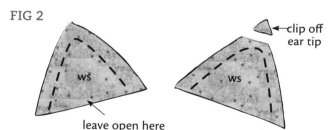

clip off ear tip

WS

WS

leave open here

FIG 1

A

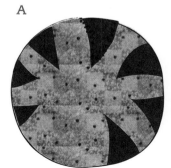

STRIPED VERSION

PATCHES VERSION

6 With the right side facing up, place the ears into position on the face (Fig 3A). Place the other piece of fabric on top with right sides together. Pin the layers together and stitch around the entire face (Fig 3B). Carefully cut a small slit through the layer of the face without the wadding (Fig 3C) and turn to the right side through the slit. Wriggle into shape and press gently.

FIG 3 A position the ears at the top

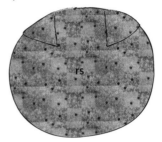

B pin and stitch together all round

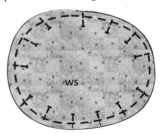

C cut a slit through one layer of fabric

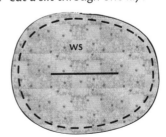

7 Using a fine-tipped fabric marking pen and the picture as a guide first draw and then embroider the details on the cat's face using backstitch and satin stitch in a contrasting colour of stranded cotton.

assembling the pincushion

8 Take the 1¾ x 13in (4.4 x 33cm) strip and join together on the short side to form a circle. With right sides together place the circle and the top of the body together, carefully pinning and then stitching together (Fig 4). Repeat with other body circle but this time leave about 2in (5cm) open. Turn the body through to the right side through this opening when stitching is complete.

FIG 4

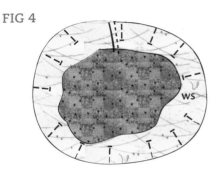

9 Firmly fill the body with toy filling and close the opening with ladder stitch. Thread a doll maker's needle with three strands of stranded embroidery cotton and knot the end. Starting at the centre of the body take a small stitch and then, with a button on the top and on the bottom, go down through the button and the body and out the other side through the button (Fig 5). Pull the thread gently but firmly to make an indentation in the pincushion and continue stitching though the buttons from front to back. Finish off the thread out of sight.

FIG 5

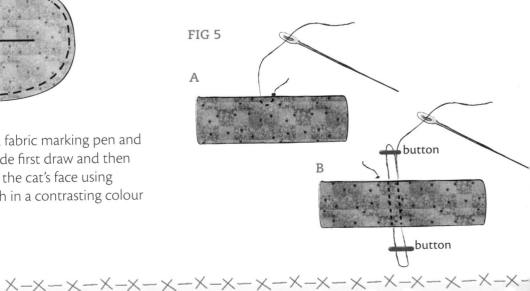

10 Position the cat's head above the paws and stitch around the head to keep it in place. I stitched from ear to ear, leaving the ears loose so they look more interesting.

best of friends

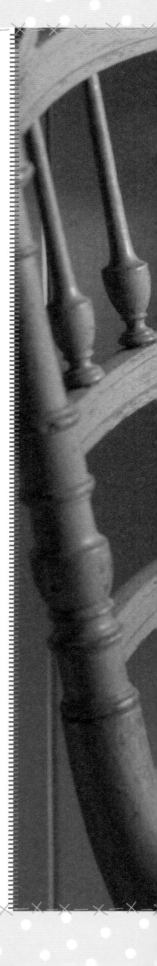

Hugo, Felix and Mr Bird make great companions for
the projects in this chapter and whether appliquéd or
embroidered they combine beautifully with crazy patchwork
to make a useful hand bag and purse. I have chosen lovely
smudgy blue-greys and raspberry reds for my hand bag. The
bag is straight forward to make, with a gusset that makes
it surprisingly roomy and a shoulder strap that can be any
length you choose. The front flap shows off the stitchery
beautifully and also draws attention to the antique button
used to fasten the bag.

The sweetest little purse with an antique-style clasp makes
a lovely companion for the hand bag and is really quick to
make, having just a small stitchery design of the three friends.

friends hand bag

This pretty bag has a crazy patchwork front and back and a shoulder strap you can make any length you like. I used needle-turn appliqué for my best friends and added yoyo flowers to the embroidery as they look so sweet and add a nice dimension to the bag. An antique celluloid button circa 1890 from my button stash makes an attractive feature on the front and is a great way to enjoy the button.

Finished size of bag, excluding strap 9½ x 9½in (24.1 x 24.1cm); embroidered flap 6 x 7½in (15.2 x 19cm) approximately.

You will need...

- 10in (25cm) square of cream-on-cream print for stitchery background

- Assorted coordinating prints for crazy patch and puffs

- Fabric scraps for cat, dog and bird appliqué

- 20in (50cm) of blue floral fabric (width of fabric) for bag strap, gusset and lining

- 10in (25cm) square of iron-on stitchery stabilizer (optional)

- DMC stranded cotton: black (310), dark brown (839), blue (926), soft green (3012) and raspberry (3721)

- 16 x 35in (40 x 90cm) of firm wadding (batting)

- 2in (5cm) wide x 40in (100cm) long (approx) thin iron-on pellon or interfacing

- Fine-tipped fabric marking pen in brown

- Button 1in (2.5cm) diameter

- Template plastic

- Light box (optional)

key for threads and stitches

The stitches used are as follows (abbreviations in brackets): backstitch (BS), satin stitch (SS), running stitch (RS), cross stitch (CS), lazy daisy (LD) and French knots (FK). See page 110 for working the stitches. Use two strands of stranded cotton unless otherwise stated.

 DMC 310 (black)
Cat's eyes, nose and mouth (BS)
String holding heart in bird's mouth (BS)
String on dog tag (BS)
Dog and bird eyes (FK)

 DMC 839 (dark brown)
Flower stems (BS)
Dog's mouth (BS)
Cat's legs, tail and inner ears (BS)
Bird's legs (BS)
Bird's beak (SS)

 DMC 926 (blue)
Bird's wing (BS)
Markings on bird's chest (BS)
Dog's collar (SS)

 DMC 3012 (soft green)
Outline of leaves (BS)
Veins on leaves (RS)

 DMC 3721 (raspberry)
Dog's heart tag (SS)
Heart hanging from bird's string (SS)

working the appliqué and stitchery

1 Use the appliqué templates on page 119 to prepare the appliqués for the dog, cat and bird. If using needle-turn appliqué as I did you will need to add ¼in (6mm) seam allowance to the shapes. Apply the shapes to the right side of the cream-on-cream fabric square.

2 Use the stitchery templates on page 120 to transfer the leaves of the flowers on to the cream-on-cream print and the animal details on to the appliqués (see page 104 for transferring designs). You could use a fine-tipped fabric marking pen to draw the parts freehand or trace them with the help of a light box.

3 Once the designs are transferred on to your fabric work the stitches. If using an iron-on stabilizer, iron it on before stitching is started. Refer to the threads and stitches key on the previous page. Once all the stitching has been completed press your work on the wrong side.

making the yoyos

4 Using template plastic make a circular template from page 119. From assorted fabrics make five yoyos following the instructions on page 107. Using the picture as a guide, stitch the yoyos in place on the stitchery.

preparing the bag pieces

5 Using the templates on page 119, make paper templates for the bag front, back and gusset. Make a template for the stitchery flap from template plastic.

6 From firm wadding (batting) cut the following pieces. Cut one piece 12 x 18in (30.5 x 46cm) and trace the bag back on to it. Cut one piece 11 x 12in (28 x 30.5cm) and trace the bag front on to it. Cut one gusset.

From blue floral fabric cut the following pieces. Cut one piece for the bag back and one for the bag back lining. Cut one piece for the bag front and one for the bag front lining. Cut two gussets – one for the bag outer and one for the lining. Cut two strips 2¼ x 35in (5.7 x 89cm) for the strap. Cut one piece 1½ x 4½in (3.8 x 11.4cm) for the button loop.

From lightweight iron-on pellon cut one strip 2¼ x 35in (5.7 x 89cm) for the strap (the seam allowance is included).

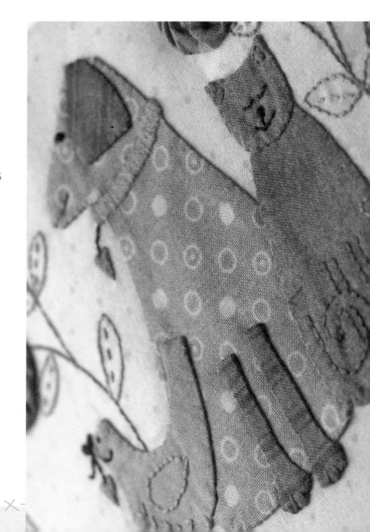

stitching the crazy patchwork

7 Starting with the bag front and choosing from the assorted coordinating prints begin with a five-sided piece of fabric, pinning it right side up in the centre of the firm wadding (Fig 1). Take another fabric strip and place right sides together on one edge of the first piece, machine stitch in place and press open. Working clockwise continue adding pieces of fabric, varying the shapes and sizes of the pieces for interest. Remember to press open after each addition. Continue adding fabric pieces until you have covered the area where the bag front has been marked, and cover over these lines to allow for the seam allowance. Press the work. Cut out the bag front, remembering to add a ¼in (6mm) seam allowance. Place aside for later.

FIG 1

12in (30.5cm)

11in (28cm)

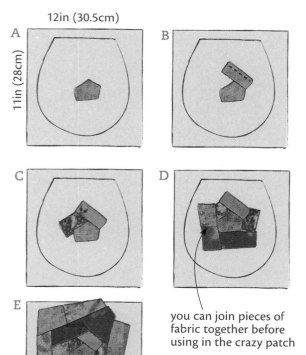

you can join pieces of fabric together before using in the crazy patch

8 Repeat the crazy patch technique for the back of the bag but stop when you get just ¼in (6mm) over the line you marked on the firm wadding – this shows where the back of the bag stops and the stitchery starts (Fig 2).

FIG 2

12in (30.5cm)

18in (47cm)

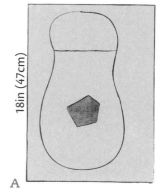

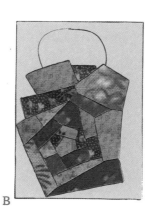

A   B

making up the bag

9 Take the completed embroidery piece and the template that you made for the front flap. Centre the template over the wrong side of the stitchery and when happy with the positioning draw around the template with a pencil. Cut out adding a ¼in (6mm) seam allowance to the flap.

10 Stitch the embroidered front flap to the back of the bag and press carefully. Cut out the bag back, remembering to add ¼in (6mm) seam allowance.

11 For the gusset, take one of the blue floral gusset pieces cut earlier and the firm wadding gusset and pin them together. Machine stitch down the centre of the gusset and add a row of stitching either side of the centre row (Fig 3).

FIG 3

12 Fold the gusset in half lengthwise and put a pin in to mark the centre. Take the front of the bag and the gusset and, with right sides together and lining up the bottom centres, carefully pin the two pieces together (Fig 4). Machine stitch the two pieces together. Clip the seam allowance. Pin and stitch the back of the bag to the gusset as for the front. Clip the seam allowance.

FIG 4

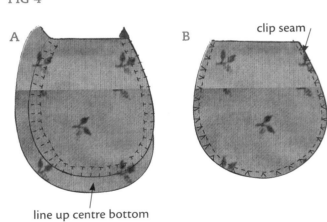

A

B

clip seam

line up centre bottom

13 Sew the lining pieces together in the same way as the bag outer, except on one side of the lining leave a 4in (10.2cm) opening at the bottom. This opening will allow you to turn the bag through to the right side once it has all been stitched together.

making the strap and loop

14 Take the two strips of blue floral cut earlier for the strap and bond the piece of lightweight iron-on pellon to the wrong side of one of the pieces. Put the two pieces right sides together and machine stitch using a ¼in (6mm) seam allowance down either edge.

15 Turn the strap through to the right side and press. Add a row of machine stitching ¼in (6mm) in from both edges – this makes the strap a bit firmer and helps to keep it in shape.

16 To make the button loop, take the piece of blue floral cut earlier. With right sides together fold it in half lengthways and stitch together with a ¼in (6mm) seam. Turn through to the right side and press to form a loop. Pin the button loop at the centre of the bag front – it needs to be facing *inwards* (Fig 5). Pin the ends of the bag strap in place (Fig 6).

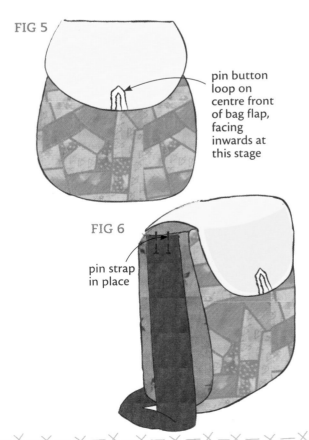

FIG 5

pin button loop on centre front of bag flap, facing inwards at this stage

FIG 6

pin strap in place

17 With right sides together put the bag outer into the bag lining. Carefully pin around all unstitched edges, matching centres and side seams. Machine stitch together.

18 Turn the bag to the right side through the opening in the bag lining. Wriggle into shape. Press the edges so the lining sits nicely out of sight. Machine stitch around the top opening and flap (see Tip below). Stitch the opening in the lining closed. Stitch your button in place and enjoy your gorgeous hand bag.

TIP
Machine stitching ⅛in (3mm) around the top opening of the bag and flap will keep the edges neat and firm.

little purse

This sweet little purse is the perfect accessory for the hand bag. It's the end of the day and these three friends are enjoying each other's company in the garden amongst the flowers. The antiqued purse frame sets this stitchery scene off nicely.
Finished size 5 x 5in (12.7 x 12.7cm) approximately.

You will need...

- 8in (20cm) square of cream-on-cream print for stitchery

- 8in (20cm) square of blue print for purse back and lining

- 8in (20cm) square of iron-on stitchery stabilizer (optional)

- DMC stranded cotton:
  black (310),
  dark brown (839),
  soft green (3012),
  raspberry (3721)
  and blue (3768)

- Purse clasp – mine was 3½in (9cm) deep x 4in (10.2cm) wide

- Lightweight iron-on pellon

- Fine-tipped fabric marking pen in brown

- Light box (optional)

working the stitchery

1 Trace the stitchery design from page 120 on to a sheet of paper. Place t design on to a light box or bright window, taped in place to prevent it moving. Place the cream fabric right side up on top and use a fine-tipped pe trace the design on to the fabric. Once the design is transferred begin workin stitches. If using an iron-on stabilizer, iron it on before stitching is started.

key for threads and stitches

The stitches used are as follows, with abbreviations in brackets: backstitch (BS), satin stitch (SS), blanket stitch (BlS), cross stitch (CS), running stitch (RS) and French knots (FK). See page 110 for how to work the various stitches. Use two strands of thread unless otherwise stated.

 DMC 310 (black)
Outline of cat (BS)
Cat's eyes, nose and mouth (BS one strand)
String for heart in bird's mouth (BS one strand)
Dog and bird eyes (FK)
Dog's mouth (BS)

 DMC 839 (dark brown)
Outline of dog (BS)
Spots on dog (SS)
Crosses on dog (CS)
Stems (BS)
Bird's legs (BS)

 DMC 3012 (soft green)
Outline of leaves (BS)
Veins on leaves (RS)

 DMC 3721 (raspberry)
Flowers (BlS)
Dog's heart tag (SS)
Heart hanging from bird's string (SS)

 DMC 3768 (blue)
Outline of bird and wing (BS)
Markings on bird's tail (RS)
Dog's collar (SS)
Flower centres (FK)

preparing the purse pieces

2 Cut out the template for the purse from template plastic, remembering to add a ¼in (6mm) seam allowance. Place the template over the completed purse front, lining up the markings with the bottom of your embroidery. You will notice there is slightly more space above the embroidery at the top of the purse – this is to allow for the purse clasp. Draw around the template and cut out on the line.

3 From the print fabric cut three pieces using the purse template – one is for the back of the purse and the other two are for the purse lining. From lightweight iron-on pellon cut two using the purse template.

sewing the purse outer and the lining

4 Now place the iron-on pellon on to the wrong side of one of the print fabric pieces and on to the wrong side of the stitchery. Fuse the pellon into place with a hot iron following the manufacturer's instructions.

TIP
Be prepared to make many more of these little purses (and the hand bag too), because when your friends see how sweet they are they will all want one!

5 Place the print fabric/pellon piece right sides together with the completed stitchery piece and pin together. Machine stitch using a ¼in (6mm) seam from (a) to (b) – see Fig 1. Turn to the right side and press gently.

FIG 1

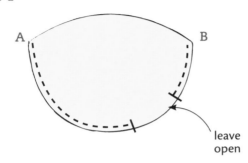

A   B

leave open

6 Take the two remaining print pieces and with right sides together, and using a ¼in (6mm) seam, machine stitch from (a) to (b), leaving an opening about 2½in (6.3cm) in one side.

assembling the purse

7 Place the purse outer inside the purse lining (Fig 2). Pin the top edges together, matching the side seams. Stitch the purse outer and the lining together using a ¼in (6mm) seam allowance. Turn through to the right side through the opening left in the purse lining (Fig 3). Stitch the opening in the lining closed. Wriggle the purse into the correct shape and press where necessary.

FIG 2

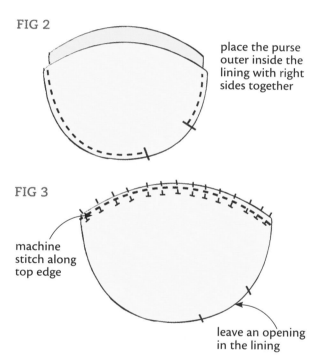

place the purse outer inside the lining with right sides together

FIG 3

machine stitch along top edge

leave an opening in the lining

8 To attach the purse clasp begin by running a gathering stitch along the top edge of the purse – it does not need to be gathered very much, just enough to ease it into the clasp. Using three strands of DMC blue (3768) and starting at the centre front, hide the starting knot in the lining and come through from the back to the front and go through the centre hole in the purse clasp. You should be able to tuck the top edge of the purse under the rim of the clasp. In backstitch work your way to one edge, end off the thread and return to the centre and stitch the other half, repeating for the other half of the clasp. Remove the gathering stitches and your little purse is now complete.

summer holiday

This chapter features an utterly charming lap quilt, which is the perfect size to have on your knees for a car journey on your way somewhere exciting. The quilt shows five appliquéd and stitched images of Hugo, Felix and Mr Bird off on their summer holidays. The adorable trio have packed their bags, loaded the car and are ready to go. We find them later relaxing outside their caravan, having a sunset picnic on the beach and, of course, building the inevitable sandcastle. Simple one-patch and nine-patch blocks alternating with the embroidered blocks, plus two easy borders make this a project you will really enjoy stitching.

There is also a great album cover to make, which would be perfect for all your holiday snapshots. It is shown with a stitchery block of the three friends off on their journey but you could stitch one of the four other designs used in the quilt instead if you prefer.

holiday fun lap quilt

In this delightful quilt we find the three friends enjoying their summer holiday. The design is an arrangement of five different stitchery blocks with four combination blocks of nine-patch and one-patch. The stitchery blocks are framed with triangles created by English paper piecing. An inner border and a pieced outer border complete the quilt. Fabrics listed below are across the width of the fabric, unless otherwise stated.

Finished size 35 x 35in (89 x 89cm) approximately.

You will need...

- 24in (60cm) cream-on-cream print for stitchery backgrounds

- 8in (20cm) each of fifteen assorted print fabrics

- 8in (20cm) of green check for inner border

- 8in (20cm) of blue print for binding

- 24in (60cm) iron-on stabilizer

- DMC stranded cotton: black (310), old gold (729), green (3011), soft red (3721), blue (3768), brown (3781) and white

- Fine-tipped permanent fabric marking pen

- Lightweight card for paper piecing (see Suppliers)

- 42 x 42in (106 x 106cm) of backing fabric

- 42 x 42in (106 x 106cm) of wadding (batting)

- Light box (optional)

preparing the stitchery designs

1 From the cream-on-cream print cut five 11in (28cm) squares – these will be trimmed down to 9½in (24.1cm) after the stitchery and appliqué has been completed.

2 Use the templates on pages 121–125 to transfer the designs on to the right side of the cream-on-cream prints (see page 104 for transferring designs). Note that the templates for each block need to be used in a specific order: first trace Template A on to the background fabric; second, use the appliqué templates to do the appliqué and third, trace the stitchery design in Template B after the appliqué has been done.

3 Using needle-turn appliqué (see page 105), apply the appropriate pieces for each block, remembering to add ¼in (6mm) seam allowance all around each piece.

working the embroideries

4 Once the designs are transferred to the fabric begin working the stitches using the keys on pages 82–86. If using an iron-on stabilizer, iron it on before stitching is started. Use two strands of DMC stranded cotton (unless otherwise stated) in the colours given in the keys. The stitches used are as follows (abbreviations in brackets): backstitch (BS), cross stitch (CS), French knots (FK), lazy daisy (LD), long stitch (LS), long and short stitch (L&S), running stitch (RS) and satin stitch (SS). See page 110 for how to work the various stitches. When the embroideries are complete gently press on the wrong side.

almost packed block – key for threads and stitches

Stitches used: backstitch (BS), cross stitch (CS), French knots (FK), lazy daisy (LD), long stitch (LS), long and short stitch (L&S), running stitch (RS) and satin stitch (SS).

 DMC 310 (black)
Musical notes (BS & FK)
Dog's eye and mouth (FK & BS)
Corner supports on suitcase (BS & FK)

 DMC 729 (old gold)
Suitcase lining (RS & BS)
Segment joining point on ball (SS)

 DMC 3721 (soft red)
Dog's collar and heart (SS)
Hearts on quilt (SS)
Spades (BS)

 DMC 3011 (green)
Bucket in suitcase (BS)
Lines on ball (BS)

 DMC 3768 (blue)
Outline and lines on quilt (BS)
Outline of ball (BS)
Mr Bird (BS & RS)

 DMC 3781 (brown)
Suitcase and handle (BS)
Cat's ears and top of head behind suitcase (BS)
Dog's bone (BS)
Mr Bird's eye, beak and legs (BS & BS)
Outline of block (BS)

on the road block – key for threads and stitches

Stitches used: backstitch (BS), cross stitch (CS), French knots (FK), lazy daisy (LD), long stitch (LS), long and short stitch (L&S), running stitch (RS) and satin stitch (SS).

 DMC 310 (black)
Bird's eye (FK)
Cat's claws, eyes, mouth and nose (BS, one strand)
Dog's eye and mouth (BS & FK)
Road markings (RS)
Inner exhaust pipe circle (BS)
String tie on luggage tag (BS)

 DMC 729 (old gold)
Bird cage (BS)
Luggage tag (SS)
Dog's name tag (SS)
Outer circle of exhaust pipe (BS)

 DMC 3011 (green)
Dashed lines along road edge (RS)
Leaves on tree (LD)
Outline of block (BS)

 DMC 3721 (soft red)
Heart on number plate (SS)

 DMC 3768 (blue)
Dog's collar (SS)
Blossoms on tree (FK)
Outline of bird (BS)
Handle on suitcase (BS)

 DMC 3781 (brown)
Outline of cat (BS)
Tree trunk and branches (BS)
Outline of dog's body (BS)
Paw print on number plate (BS)
Edge of the road (BS)

sunset picnic block – key for threads and stitches

Stitches used: backstitch (BS), cross stitch (CS), French knots (FK), lazy daisy (LD), long stitch (LS), long and short stitch (L&S), running stitch (RS) and satin stitch (SS).

 DMC 310 (black)
Paw prints (SS)
Cat (L&S)
Fish skeleton (SS & BS, one strand)
Lines on dog's patch (LS)

 DMC 729 (old gold)
Sun and sun rays (BS)
Basket (BS)

 DMC 3011 (green)
Bottle (BS)
Cork in bottle (SS)

 DMC 3721 (soft red)
Dog's collar (SS)
Blossom in tree (FK)
Dog's heart tag (SS)
Line and fringing on blanket (BS)

 DMC 3768 (blue)
Top line of the ocean (BS)
Waves in ocean (BS)
Birds in tree (BS)

 DMC 3781 (brown)
Tree trunk and branches (BS)
Dog's ears (SS)
Dog's bone (BS)
Dashed line under field edge (BS)

 DMC Blanc (white)
Tips of cat's ears and tail (SS)

at the campsite block – key for threads and stitches

Stitches used: backstitch (BS), cross stitch (CS), French knots (FK), lazy daisy (LD), long stitch (LS), long and short stitch (L&S), running stitch (RS) and satin stitch (SS).

 DMC 310 (black)
Tyres (BS)
Chimney on caravan (BS)
Tow bar (BS)
Tie on dog's shorts (BS)
Window frames (BS)
Door screen outline (BS)
Door screen inner (RS)
Dog's eye (FK)
Dog's mouth (BS)
Cat's eyes, nose and mouth (BS)
Writing on cat bowl (BS)

 DMC 3011 (green)
Line of grass (BS)
Dashed lines under line of grass (RS)
Flower stems (BS)

 DMC 3781(brown)
Dog (BS)
Cat (BS)
Outline of block (BS)

 DMC 3721 (soft red)
Curtains (BS)
Alternate spots on dog's shorts (SS)
Flowers (FK)
Milk tankard (BS)
Heart tag on dog's collar (SS)

 DMC 729 (old gold)
Deckchair frame (BS)
Hubcap on caravan (LS)
Alternate spots on dog's shorts (SS)

 DMC 3768 (blue)
Bird (BS & RS)
Outline of dog's shorts (BS)
Dog's collar (SS)
Cat's bowl (BS)

day at the beach block - key for threads and stitches

Stitches used: backstitch (BS), cross stitch (CS), French knots (FK), lazy daisy (LD), long stitch (LS), long and short stitch (L&S), running stitch (RS) and satin stitch (SS).

 DMC 310 (black)
Bird's eye (FK)
Cat's eyes, mouth and nose (BS, one strand)
Dog's eye and mouth (FK & BS)
Dog's name tag (SS)
Crab's eyes (FK)
Paw print on flag (BS)
Flag pole (BS)

 DMC 729 (old gold)
Sun (FK in centre and then BS)
Sun rays (RS)
Top line of sand (BS)
Dots on sand (FK)
Flower centres on bird's shorts (FK)
Bird's legs and beak (BS)
Outline of block (BS)

 DMC 3011 (green)
Bucket (BS)

 DMC 3721 (soft red)
Dog's collar (SS)
Spade (BS)
Outline and flowers on bird's shorts (BS & LD)

 DMC 3768 (blue)
Outline of flag (BS)
Windows on sandcastle (BS)
Rubber ring (BS & SS)
Mr Bird (BS & RS)

 DMC 3781 (brown)
Outline of cat and coat markings (BS)
Outline of dog's body (BS)

making the framing border

5 Now the embroidery is finished you can create a frame for the blocks using English paper piecing (see page 106). Using the triangle template below (Fig 1) and lightweight card create 180 card templates. Make one more card template but this time add a ¼in (6mm) seam allowance all round – this will make the triangle template size 2⅛in (5.3cm) at the base (Fig 2). Use this template to cut 180 triangles from assorted prints.

FIG 1 triangle template (actual size)

FIG 2

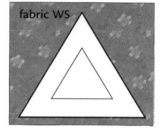

larger card template with ¼in (6mm) seam allowance

6 Using the smaller card triangles, place one on the wrong side of a fabric triangle, fold the seam allowance over on to the card and tack (baste) to the card all round. Keep the fabric firm and tuck in all points neatly (Fig 3). Do this with all the triangles.

7 Using the corner template below (Fig 4) and the lightweight card create twenty card templates. Make one more card template but this time add a ¼in (6mm) seam allowance all round as you did for the other template. Use this template to cut twenty corners from assorted prints.

FIG 4 corner template (actual size)

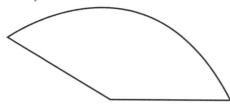

8 Using the smaller corner card shapes, place one of the templates on the wrong side of one of the fabric pieces and fold the seam allowance over on to the card and tack (baste) to the card all round. Do this with all the corners.

9 Place two fabric-covered triangles right sides together and stitch together using small whip stitches. Take care not to stitch through the card. Stitch nine triangles together and then add a corner. Continue in this way until the framing border is complete and then press well. Carefully remove the card templates and place the border in position around the embroidery. Pin in place and then stitch in place with a blind hem stitch. Press well. Make a framing border for each embroidered block.

FIG 3

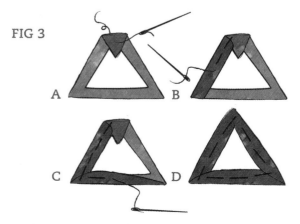

FIG 5

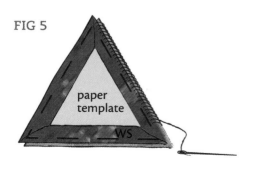

making the nine-patch and one-patch blocks

10 From assorted fabrics cut a total of 180 1½in (3.8cm) squares. Using a ¼in (6mm) seam allowance sew the nine-patch blocks together (see Fig 6). You need to make a total of twenty of these blocks. For the one-patch blocks use your assorted prints and cut a total of sixteen 3½in (8.9cm) squares.

FIG 6

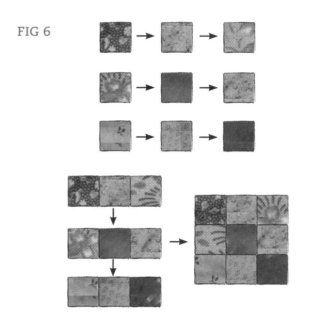

11 Take five of the nine-patch and four of the one-patch blocks and sew together as in Fig 7. Make four of these joining blocks in total. The block finished size is 9½in (24.1cm) square including seam allowance.

FIG 7

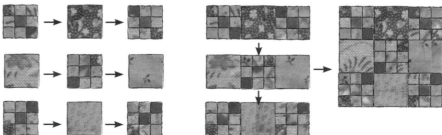

The layout of this Holiday Fun lap quilt is very simple but effective.
The triangular framing borders around the stitcheries turn them into
lovely focal points. Children will love a bedtime story based around
the adventures of the three friends on this quilt.

assembling the quilt and adding the borders

12 Cut each of the embroidered blocks down to 9½in (24.1cm) square (this measurement includes seam allowance). Using the picture on the previous page as a guide and a ¼in (6mm) seam allowance join all the blocks of the quilt together.

13 For the inner border use the inner border fabric and cut two 2 x 27½in (5 x 70cm) strips for the top and bottom borders and two 2 x 30½in (5 x 77.5cm) strips for the side borders. Join the top and bottom borders to the quilt first, and then add the side borders, using ¼in (6mm) seam allowances. Press the completed top.

> **TIP**
> Before cutting the fabric for the borders check the measurement of your own quilt, in case it differs from mine.

14 For the outer border use assorted fabrics to cut a total of sixty-four 2½in (6.3cm) squares. Select fifteen of these squares and join them together for the top outer border, using ¼in (6mm) seam allowances. Repeat for the bottom border. Join the top and bottom borders to the main quilt. Now select seventeen of the 2½in (6.3cm) squares and join them together for the left side outer border. Repeat for the right side outer border. Join these side borders to the quilt.

quilting and finishing

15 Make a quilt sandwich from the quilt top, wadding (batting) and backing, as described on page 108 and quilt your work. Bind the quilt to finish – see page 109 for instructions. My quilt was hand quilted as follows.

- Outline quilting very close to all the main embroidered motifs and around the outer backstitched line of the blocks.
- Simple heart shapes in the one-patch blocks (see template below), with a cross pattern from corner to corner of the nine-patch blocks.
- A double heart pattern in the inner border with a cross in each corner (template below).

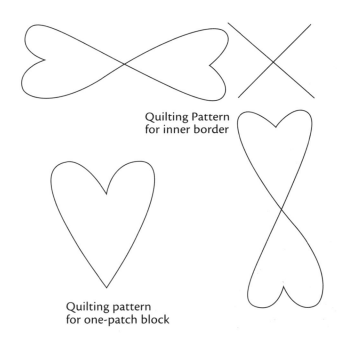

Quilting Pattern for inner border

Quilting pattern for one-patch block

Enlarge all templates by 166.6% to full size

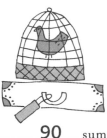

photo album

A soft-cover photo album is a wonderful way to display photos from a special holiday. The delightful picture on the front is a combination of embroidery, appliqué and English paper piecing. It shows the three friends on the road, which is the same block used in the quilt, but you could stitch one of the other scenes instead.
Finished size of stitchery block 9½ x 9½in (24.1 x 24.1cm).

You will need...

- Photo album – mine is 14in (35.5cm) square

- 32in (81cm) of red print for album cover and lining

- 12in (30.5cm) square of cream linen

- Scraps of fifteen assorted prints for appliqué and border

- DMC stranded cotton: black (310), old gold (729), green (3011), soft red (3721), blue (3768), brown (3781) and white

- Fine-tipped permanent fabric marking pen

- Lightweight card for paper piecing (see Suppliers)

- 12in (30.5cm) square of iron-on stabilizer (optional)

- 16in (40.5cm) lightweight iron-on pellon or interfacing

- Light box (optional)

preparing the stitchery design

1 Using the On the Road templates on page 122, transfer the design on to the right side of the square of cream linen (see page 104 for transferring designs). Note that the templates need to be used in a specific order: first trace Template A on to the background fabric; second, use the appliqué templates to do the appliqué and third, trace the stitchery design in Template B after the appliqué has been done.

2 Using needle-turn appliqué (see page 105), apply the appropriate pieces, remembering to add ¼in (6mm) seam allowance around each piece.

working the stitchery

3 Once the designs are transferred on to your fabric begin working the stitches. If using an iron-on stabilizer, iron it on before the stitching is started. Refer to page 83 for stitchery instructions.

4 Once all the stitching is completed gently press your work on the wrong side. Trim the stitchery down to 10¼in (26cm) square. Turn under approximately ¼in (6mm) all around the stitchery, tack (baste) in place and then press.

making the framing border

5 Make the framing border using English paper piecing as described in steps 5–9 on page 87.

making the album cover

6 The size of your photo album will govern what size you need to cut your fabrics. So measure your photo album from cover edge to cover edge and add about 4in (10.2cm) on each end for the turn-backs. My album measured 28 x 13⅝in (71.1 x 49cm) so from red print I cut two pieces 36½ x 14½in (92.7 x 36.8cm).

7 Fuse the pellon on to the wrong side of one of the 36½ x 14½in (92.7 x 36.8cm) pieces of fabric. Place the album cover outer and the lining right sides together and with a ¼in (6mm) seam stitch around the rectangle leaving an opening so you can turn it through to the right side (Fig 1). Clip corners, turn through to the right side and press so the lining is not visible from the front. Slip stitch the opening closed.

FIG 1

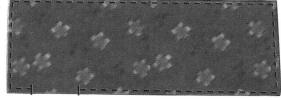

8 Place the rectangle around the album and fold the turn-backs to the inside. Pin in place, with an even amount back and front. Slide the cover off and stitch the turn-backs in place (Fig 2).

FIG 2

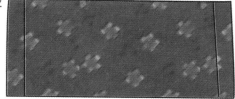

9 Put the cover on the album and centre the embroidered block on the front. Once you are happy with the position pin it in place. Remove the cover from the album and attach the stitchery to the cover with blind hem stitch. Put the cover back on the album to finish.

forever friends

My dog Hugo and my cat Felix are constant companions. Ever since they were little they have done everything together, whether they are playing in the garden, bug hunting, sharing a bowl of water or sleeping they can be found side by side. The charming little wall hanging project in this chapter shows this endearing companionship.

The wall hanging uses a technique called punch needle embroidery, where a thread is punched through fabric with a hollow pencil-shaped needle, which leaves tufted loops on top of the fabric. It's a bit like rug hooking but the resulting embroidery has more detail. It's great fun to do and can be used as a companion to patchwork and appliqué. I used walnut ink on my finished piece to create a lovely aged look.

A handy box, shown on page 100, also uses the punch needle technique, this time showing Hugo with his other friend, Mr Bird. I've used a circular wooden box but you could choose a different container if you wish.

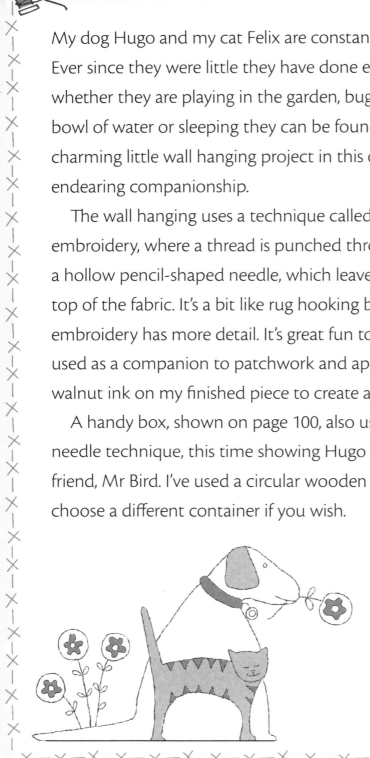

friends wall hanging

This punch needle embroidery wall hanging shows my dog Hugo and his best friend Felix sharing a day together in the garden. Strong colours and texture come together to make this delightful project. The wall hanging uses weaver's cloth, which is rather like linen or heavy muslin but which is more suited to punch needle work.
Finished size 6¼ x 4¼in (16 x 11cm) approximately.

You will need...

- 12in (30cm) square of weaver's cloth (see Suppliers)

- 6 x 8in (15.2 x 20.3cm) of wool fabric for backing

- DMC stranded cottons: black (310), dark red (815), dark olive green (935), pale stone (3033), stone (3032), plum (3740), dark brown (3781), dark teal blue (3808), old gold (3829) and ecru

- Black wool yarn with a slub or loops for edging

- Cameo Ultra Punch™ tool

- Fine-tipped fabric marking pen

- Light box (optional)

- 7in (18cm) diameter locking-lip embroidery hoop

- 12in (30.5cm) length of twine for hanger

- Walnut ink for aging (or use tea-dyeing)

transferring the design

1 Use the template on page 126. Take the weaver's cloth and trace the punch needle design in the centre (it doesn't matter which side), using a fine-tipped fabric marking pen and a light source such as a light box or window. The template has the design drawn in *reverse* because with punch needle embroidery you work from the back to the front of the design.

2 Once the design has been transferred on to the cloth put it into the embroidery hoop. You need to have your work drum tight in the hoop but make sure as you tighten the hoop that you do not distort the design.

working the embroidery

3 You are now ready to get punching. On this design I used six strands of DMC stranded cotton due to the large size of some of the areas that need filling. These instructions are for the Cameo tool. If using a different one refer to the manufacturer's instructions. Thread the Cameo Ultra Punch needle as shown in Fig 1A–E: there are two parts to the gadget – the punch needle and the threader (Fig 1A). First adjust the needle to a number one setting, which will give the shortest loop. Put the threader into the needle tip and feed it through the hollow needle until it comes out the handle end (1B). Slip the thread into the folded end of the wire and slowly pull the threader back through the needle (1C). Once the thread appears at the needle tip you can remove the thread from the threader. Thread the eye of the needle from the back or rounded side, through to the slanted front side. Insert the threader from the back to the front of the eye and place the thread into the wire threader (1D). Pull the threader back through the eye of the needle, then remove the thread, leaving a little tail about 1in (2.5cm) long (1E).

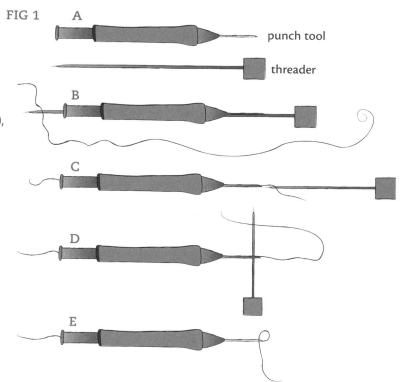

FIG 1

A — punch tool
— threader

B

C

D

E

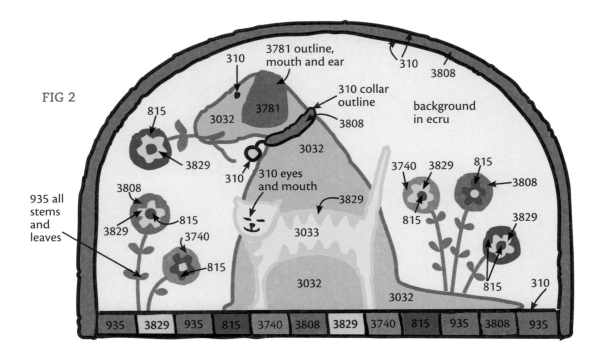

FIG 2

3781 outline, mouth and ear

310

310

3808

815

3032

3781

310 collar outline

3808

background in ecru

3032

3740

3829

815

3808

3829

310

310 eyes and mouth

3829

815

3808

815

3829

935 all stems and leaves

3829

3833

3740

815

3829

3033

3740

815

3032

3032

3032

815

310

935	3829	935	815	3740	3808	3829	3740	815	935	3808	935

4 Generally, start work at the centre of the design and work your way outwards, leaving the background until last. You should be working on the wrong (back) side of your work and on this side the stitches will look like tiny running stitches. Follow the thread codes and colours in Fig 2.

5 Hold the needle in an upright position as you would a pen, with the front/slant of the needle facing the same direction as your thumbnail (Fig 3A). I rest my hoop on the edge of a table to ensure that I do not stab myself with the needle, which is very sharp. Having decided where you are going to start, brush the thread tail to one side and have the length of thread flowing freely over the top of your hand, because if the thread gets caught on anything it will undo the loops as you make them, which is annoying! Carefully push the needle into the fabric in a punching action, until the hilt of the needle prevents it from going further (3B). Gently pull the needle out until the tip is just on the surface of the fabric (3C) and then slide the needle across the fabric surface and punch the next stitch close to the first stitch (3D). Continue adding stitches using this punch-lift-slide method, making sure that each stitch is punched to the hilt of the needle, which will ensure that the loops are a consistent height. Take your time and concentrate

on getting the technique right – you will get faster with practise. Don't panic when you take a peek at the right side of the work: in the early stages the loops look floppy but as the design builds up the loops start holding each other up.

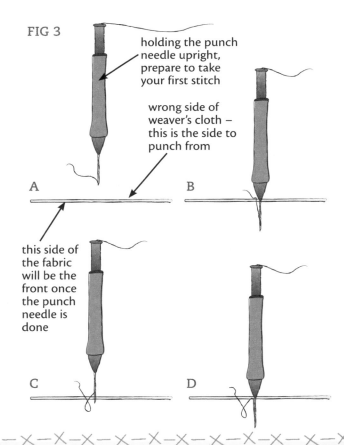

FIG 3

holding the punch needle upright, prepare to take your first stitch

wrong side of weaver's cloth – this is the side to punch from

A

B

this side of the fabric will be the front once the punch needle is done

C

D

TIP

If you lift the needle out too far you will not only have varying lengths of loops on the front of your work but will also have small loops on the back of your work – which is not the end of the world but is not correct.

6 Once you have completed an area and want to finish off or change a colour put your work down on a flat surface, leaving the needle in the fabric. Place a finger from your free hand over the area where the needle is, apply a little pressure and slowly lift the needle out of the work. When you have about 1in (2.5cm) of thread showing, remove your finger and with sharp embroidery scissors, snip the thread off flush with the surface. You can trim off the starting tail of thread now or earlier if it's getting in the way. You don't need to knot anything as the work will not come undone.

7 Once you have completed your piece remove it from the embroidery hoop. Gently press the cloth around the design to remove the ring left by the hoop.

ageing the embroidery

8 I aged my embroidery by spraying it with diluted walnut ink. In a small spray bottle mix about one part ink to four parts water and shake well. Place the embroidery on waste paper to protect the surrounding area. Spray the mixture straight on to the embroidery – it will soak in. Have a piece of kitchen paper handy to dab the work and lift some of the spray out if it looks too dark. Dry the embroidery in a warm place for about twenty minutes.

assembling the wall hanging

9 Trim the cloth back to within ½in (1.3cm) of the embroidery. Turn the excess cloth to the wrong side of the work and press to keep in place.

10 On a flat surface place the punched piece right side down. Position the black wool yarn around the edge, tucking the beginning and the end of the yarn out of sight (Fig 4). Use black sewing thread to stitch the yarn in place.

FIG 4

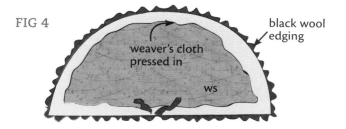

weaver's cloth pressed in

black wool edging

ws

11 Using the punched piece as a template cut a piece of wool backing. Place the punched piece and the backing wrong sides together and position the length of twine for the hanger (see Fig 5). Stitch the twine in place taking care not to stitch through to the front of the work. Hand stitch the backing in place to finish.

FIG 5

punch needle box

A simple wooden box can be turned into an heirloom item with the addition of a punch needle embroidery lid. The design of Hugo, with his favourite blanket and his friend Mr Bird, is smaller than the wall hanging design and would be a good project to practise your punch needle skills.

Finished size 6in (15.2cm) diameter.

You will need...

- 12in (30cm) square of weaver's cloth (see Suppliers)

- DMC stranded cottons: variegated red (115), black (310), old gold (729), burnt orange (919), country blue (931), moss green (936), green (3011), pale stone (3033), dirt brown (3781), biscuit (3828) and ginger (3829)

- DMC Linen thread in fawn (4145)

- Lopi decorative black yarn for around edge of punch needle

- Cameo Ultra Punch™ tool

- Fine-tipped marking pen

- Light box (optional)

- 7in (18cm) diameter locking-lip embroidery hoop

- Wooden box – mine was 6in (15.2cm) diameter x 2¾in (7cm) high

- Walnut ink (for aging process)

- Craft glue

transferring the design

1 Use the template on page 126. Take the weaver's cloth and trace the punch needle design in the centre (it doesn't matter which side), using a fine-tipped fabric marking pen and a light source such as a light box or window. The template has the design drawn in *reverse* because with punch needle embroidery you work from the back to the front.

2 Once the design has been transferred on to the cloth you can put it into the embroidery hoop. You need to have your work drum tight in the hoop but make sure as you tighten the hoop that you do not distort the design.

working the embroidery

3 You are now ready to get punching. On this box lid design I used two strands of DMC stranded cotton and set my punch needle on the number 1 setting. Follow the colours and codes shown in Fig 1.

4 To work the punch needle embroidery follow steps 3–6 on pages 97–99 for the technique. Once the work is finished remove it from the embroidery hoop. Gently press the cloth around the design to remove the ring left by the hoop. I aged my embroidery with diluted walnut ink – see step 8 on page 99 for instructions.

finishing the box

5 Trim the cloth to within ½in (1.3cm) of the embroidery. Turn the excess cloth to the wrong side of the work and use craft glue to keep it in place.

6 Place the embroidered circle on your box lid and mark the edge all round with a pencil. Draw a thin line of glue just outside this edge all round and glue a length of black wool along this line. Spread more glue on the rest of the box top, inside the black wool, and put your embroidered circle into position, pressing it down firmly to make good contact with the glue. Adjust the back wool edging so it is snug up against the embroidery all round.

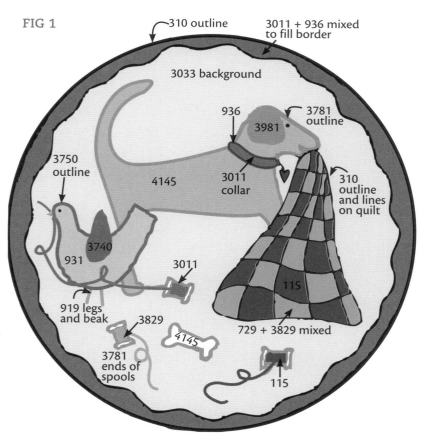

FIG 1

310 outline

3011 + 936 mixed to fill border

3033 background

936

3981

3781 outline

3750 outline

4145

3011 collar

310 outline and lines on quilt

3740

931

3011

919 legs and beak

3781 ends of spools

4145

115

729 + 3829 mixed

115

materials and equipment

materials

The projects each have a list of the materials and equipment required and the basics are described here, but there's no reason why you can't experiment, especially with fabrics and embellishments.

fabrics and wadding (batting)

For many people 100% cotton fabrics are the ones of choice for patchwork and quilting but sometimes it is great to try other fabrics. The fabrics used to back quilts, bind quilts or to line projects such as bags can really be anything you like but cotton is the easiest to handle.

Quilt wadding (batting) is rated by its weight and is sold in standard sizes and by the yard or metre. It is available in polyester, cotton, wool and various blends and for hand and machine quilting. Thinner wadding tends to be used when machine quilting. I prefer to use Matilda's Own Wool/poly blend, which is pre-washed, pre-shrunk, fully machine washable and comes in white and charcoal. I used Matilda's Own Bamboo in the Summer Holiday quilt, which was nice to work with and has a very soft handle. The bamboo is eco-friendly and grows without the use of irrigation or insecticides.

threads

Many people like to use 100% cotton thread for machine piecing and machine quilting. Polyester mixes are also popular. Threads for hand quilting can be almost anything you like. If you want the quilting to blend or tone with the fabrics then use a cotton or polyester.

For my stitcheries I use DMC stranded cottons. These are in six-stranded skeins that can be split into separate strands and are available the world over in a very wide range of colours.

fusible web and interfacing

Fusible web is also referred to as iron-on adhesive and is an ultra-thin sheet of adhesive backed with a special paper. When the web is placed between two fabrics, the heat of an iron causes the glue to melt and fuse the fabrics together – perfect for appliqué (see page 105 for fusible web appliqué.) There are various makes of fusible web, including Bondaweb (Vliesofix or Wonder Under) and Steam-A-Seam2. Read the manufacturer's instructions before use.

Fusible interfacing or pellon works on the same principle but is single-sided. It is used to stiffen and strengthen fabrics. An iron-on stabilizer can be used to strengthen a fabric, making it more able to support embroidery stitches. It needs to be ironed on before the stitching is started.

buttons

I like to use buttons in my work, not just functional ones, such as the antique one used on the hand bag on page 68 but also to represent animals' eyes and flower centres. I now have my own range of buttons, such as the dog button used in the needle case on page 18 – see Suppliers on page 127.

craft glue

A few projects use a fast-tack (quick-setting) craft glue to fix pieces of the project together. Always use a glue that is suitable for fabric and make sure to follow the instructions on the packet and use in a well ventilated room.

paint

I used paint for the Cat Lover Wall Quilt and like Jo Sonja paint, which can be mixed with a textile medium. I have found that as long as you set the paint with the heat of an iron it is stable. There are other craft paints available but test them first on a scrap of fabric.

equipment

There are many pieces of equipment and gadgets you could buy for patchwork and quilting but a basic tool kit is all you really need to start with.

basic tool kit
- Quilter's ruler
- Rotary cutter
- Cutting mat
- Tape measure
- Needles
- Pins
- Thimble
- Scissors
- Template plastic
- Marking pen
- Iron
- Sewing machine
- Roxanne Glue Baste-It™
- Cameo Ultra Punch™ tool
- Embroidery hoop with locking lip

rotary cutter, ruler and mat

Patchwork is made so much easier by the use of a rotary cutter, ruler and mat, especially for quilt making. You will find a self-healing cutting mat 18in x 24in is very useful and a 45mm or 60mm diameter rotary cutter.

pins and needles

You will need pins for piecing patchwork and for fastening the layers of a quilt together. Safety pins could also be used for securing the quilt sandwich. Alternatively, spray adhesives are available for this.

You will need a selection of hand sewing needles for embroidery and quilting and machine needles for piecing and quilting. I use Clover No. 9 embroidery needles and love the smooth, quality finish the needles have. Their gold eye makes them easy to thread.

marking pens

In this book markers are mostly used to mark stitchery designs on to fabric. I use a Zig Millenium or Pigma Micron permanent marker pen, usually in brown. There are also water- and air-soluble pens that can be used to mark fabric temporarily.

template plastic

This is a transparent plastic that can be used to create durable templates which can be used over and over again. It is available from craft shops and patchwork and quilting suppliers. The template is traced on to the plastic and cut out with sharp scissors (don't use your fabric scissors!). Use a permanent marker to label the template.

light box

This is a useful piece of equipment for tracing designs but can be expensive so try using a well-lit window instead. Tape the design to the light box (or window), tape the fabric on top and trace the design on to the fabric. I also use a light under a glass table, which works well and stops my arms getting tired when standing at a window!

punch needle tool

Punch needle embroidery requires a special tool. I use the Cameo Ultra Punch tool because it is easier to thread than many others and is also comfortable to hold in your hand. Your local craft store should have punch needles or you could shop online.

basic techniques

This section describes the basic techniques you will need to make and finish off the projects in this book, from transferring designs to binding a finished quilt. Beginners should find it very useful.

sewing seams

Patchwork or pieced work does require that your seams are accurate in order that your blocks will fit together nicely. Maintaining an accurate ¼in (6mm) seam allowance where stated will give the best results. For really accurate piecing sew a *bare* ¼in (6mm) seam, as this will allow for the thickness of thread and the tiny amount of fabric taken up when the seam is pressed.

pressing work

Your work will look its best if you press it well. Generally, seams are pressed towards the darker fabric to avoid darker colours showing through on the right side. If joining seams are pressed in opposite directions they will lock together nicely and create the flattest join. Press (don't iron) and be very careful with steam, as this can stretch fabric, particularly edges cut on the bias.

using templates

The templates are given on pages 112–126 and most will need to be enlarged to full size – please read all of the instructions with each template carefully. Once a template is the size required you can trace it on to paper or thin card, cut it out and use it as a pattern to cut the shape from paper. Before cutting out check whether a ¼in (6mm) seam allowance is needed. If using a template for needle-turn appliqué a seam allowance will be required, but will not be needed if you are using a fusible web appliqué technique.

reversing templates

Sometimes it is necessary to reverse a template, so that a design will appear facing the other way. One way to reverse a template is to photocopy it and place the copy on to a light source with the template face down rather than right side up. The design is then reversed and you can trace it as normal. You could also trace the template on to tracing paper, turn the tracing paper over and trace the template again on to paper.

transferring designs

Designs can be transferred on to fabric in various ways. I use a light source, such as a light box, a window or a light under a glass table. Iron your fabric so it is free of creases. Place the design right side up and then the fabric right side up on top, taping in place if necessary. Use a fine-tipped fabric marking pen or a pencil to trace the design. If the marks might show later then use an erasable marker, such as an air-erasable or water-soluble one.

tea dyeing

To speckle tea-dye calico, as I did for my Cat Lover quilt, wet the fabric and squeeze out most of the water. Lay it flat and sprinkle generously with tea leaves (a tea bag cut open or loose tea). Long tea leaves create wonderful effects. Fold the fabric into a parcel, place on a plate, damp well and microwave on high for two minutes. It will be *hot* when you take it out, so take care. Open out and see if you like the markings, if not re-fold the parcel, damp again and repeat the cooking. When happy with the result shake off tea leaves, rinse the fabric well and iron dry. If you want a creased effect, line dry for a short while and then press.

appliqué

Appliqué is the technique of fixing one fabric shape or pattern on top of another, and can be done in various ways. I have used two methods for the projects in this book – needle-turn appliqué and fusible web appliqué.

needle-turn appliqué

This is a traditional method of hand appliqué where each appliqué piece has a seam turned under all round and is stitched into position on the background fabric. The appliqué shapes may be drawn freehand or templates used, as I have done for the designs in this book.

1 Mark the appliqué shape on the right side of your fabric and then mark another line further out all round for the seam allowance. This is usually ¼in (6mm) but may change depending on the size of the appliqué piece being stitched and type of fabric being used. Smaller pieces may only need a ⅛in (3mm) allowance to reduce bulk. Clip the seam allowance on concave curves (the inward ones) to make it easier to turn the seam under.

2 For each appliqué piece turn the seam allowance under all round and press. Position the appliqué on the background fabric and stitch into place with tiny slip stitches all round. Press the appliqué when finished. Some people like to use the needle to turn the seam under as they stitch the appliqué in place.

fusible web appliqué

Fusible web has an adhesive that melts when heated so when the web is placed between two fabrics the heat of an iron causes the fabrics to fuse together, which makes it ideal for appliqué.

1 When using templates for fusible web appliqué they need to be flipped or reversed because you will be drawing the shape on the back of the fabric – see reversing templates opposite.

2 Trace around each template on to the paper side of the fusible web, leaving about ½in (1.3cm) around each shape. Cut out roughly around each shape. Iron the fusible web, paper side up, on to the wrong side of the appliqué fabric and then cut out accurately on your drawn line.

3 When the web is cool, peel off the backing paper and place the appliqué in position on your project, right side up. Fuse into place with a medium-hot iron for about ten seconds. Allow the appliqué to cool.

4 The edge of the appliqué can be secured further by stitches. I have used blanket stitch as I like the hand-crafted look but machine satin stitch can also be used.

crazy stitch and flip

I have used this technique in several projects as it is an easy way to piece together patches for a crazy patchwork look. It is normally stitched on to a foundation fabric, such as calico and needs assorted strips or rough polygon shapes of fabric.

1 Begin at the centre of the design, or where directed in the project instructions, and pin the first strip or shape right side up on the foundation fabric (Fig 1A).

FIG 1

A

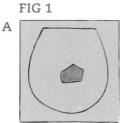

2 Place a second strip of fabric right side together with the first, aligning one edge and sew it in place (1B). Flip the second fabric over so it is now right side up and press in place.

3 Place a third fabric strip right sides together with the second piece and sew together (1C). Continue in this way to cover the whole design area (1D). The overlapping edges can then be trimmed to size.

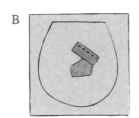

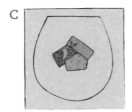

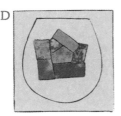

B

C

D

3 Place two fabric shapes right sides together, aligning edges and use small whip stitches to sew them together through the folded fabric, but not through the paper. Place a third fabric shape right sides together with the second and sew together. Continue building the design in this way. Once all stitching is finished remove the tacking and the papers.

FIG 2

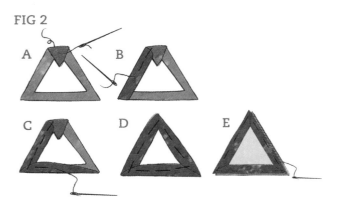

english paper piecing

This type of patchwork is also called English patchwork and uses templates, usually made of paper or thin card, which fabric pieces are wrapped around and tacked (basted) to. The patches are hand sewn together and the papers removed.

1 From a master template, create enough paper templates for the project. When cutting out the fabric pieces you need to allow for a ¼in (6mm) seam all round. Make one master template but this time add a ¼in (6mm) seam allowance all round and use this to cut out your fabric pieces.

2 Follow Fig 2A–E and pin a paper template to a fabric shape and fold the seam allowance over the edges of the template, tacking (basting) in place through all layers. Keep the fabric firm around the paper shape and tuck in all points neatly. Repeat with all the fabric pieces.

punch needle work

Punch needle embroidery is an old Russian technique that uses embroidery thread in a continuous feed system to create looped images on the surface of fabric. Thread is punched through a fabric with a hollow, pencil-shaped needle, leaving tufted loops on top of the fabric. The technique is similar to rug hooking but more intricate images can be achieved. The technique is described and illustrated on pages 97–99.

making yoyos

Yoyos are sometimes called Suffolk puffs. They are really easy to make and add a lovely three-dimensional touch to patchwork and appliqué.

1 Using a fine-tipped fabric marking pen, draw around a circular template on the wrong side of your fabrics. Cut out on the line (the seam allowance is included in the project template).

2 Thread your needle with a double strand of sewing cotton and knot one end. Take one of the circles and with the wrong side facing you fold over approximately ¼in (6mm). Make a running stitch around the entire edge (see Fig 3A below), turning the ¼in (6mm) in as you go and gathering it slightly.

3 Once you have got back to where you started, gently pull on the thread to gather it – you may need to wriggle the yoyo between your fingers to get it into shape (Fig 3B). Pull the thread firmly once you are happy with the look and tie the thread off at the back.

FIG 3

A   B

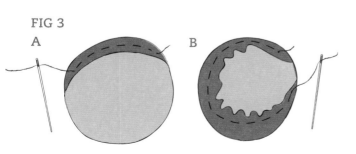

adding borders

A border frames a quilt and can tie the whole design together. Borders can be plain and simple or pieced and I have used both types in this book, all sewn on with straight or butted corners, which are very simple to do.

1 Calculate what length the border should be by measuring the width of the quilt through the centre and cut the top and bottom borders to this measurement (Fig 4A). Measuring this way is more accurate than measuring at the ends, which may have spread a little during the making of the quilt. Cut the top and bottom borders to this length and sew to the quilt top using ¼in (6mm) seams and then press.

FIG 4

A

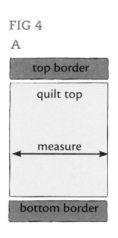

B

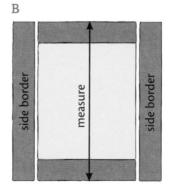

2 Measure the quilt height through the centre, including the top and bottom borders you have just added (Fig 4B). Cut the side borders to this measurement, sew them in place and press. To add a second border, repeat steps 1 and 2.

—✕—✕—✕—✕—✕—✕—✕—✕—✕—✕—✕—✕—✕—✕—✕—✕—

joining strips

Sometimes you will need to join fabric strips together to make them long enough for borders or binding. Joining them with a diagonal seam at a 45 degree angle will make them less noticeable, as will pressing the seams open (Fig 5).

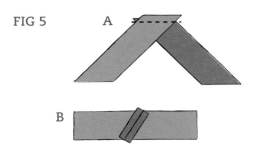

FIG 5

making a quilt sandwich

A quilt sandwich is a term often used to describe the three layers of a quilt – the top, the wadding (batting) and the backing. These layers need to be secured together so that a quilt will hang correctly and be free of puckers. Any hand or machine quilting you plan to do will look much better if the quilt layers are secured well.

1 Press your backing fabric and hang out your wadding if necessary to reduce creases. Cut out your wadding and backing about 4in (10.2cm) larger all round than the quilt top. Prepare the quilt top by cutting off or tying in any stray ends, pressing it and sorting out your seam allowances so they lay as flat as possible.

2 Lay the backing fabric right side down on a smooth surface and tape the corners to keep it flat. Put the wadding (batting) on top, smoothing out any wrinkles. Now put the quilt top right side up on top.

3 Securing the three layers together can be done in various ways, for example, some people use pins or safety pins, some use tacking (basting), others use a spray glue. If using pins or tacking then use a grid pattern, spacing the lines out about 3–6in (7.6–15.2cm) apart. Tack the outside edges of the quilt sandwich too, about ½in (1.3cm) in from the edge. The sandwich is now ready for quilting.

quilting

Quilting not only adds texture and interest to a quilt but also secures all the layers together. I have used a combination of hand and machine quilting on the projects in this book. The hand quilting stitch is really just a running stitch and ideally the length of the stitches and the spaces in between need to be small and even. Machine quilting has a more continuous look and the stitch length is usually about 10–12 stitches per 1in (2.5cm) and may depend on the fabric and threads you are using. How much or how little quilting you do is up to you but aim for a fairly even amount over the whole quilt. When starting and finishing hand or machine quilting, the starting knot and the thread end need to be hidden in the wadding (batting). I have described within the projects where I quilted the projects in this book. Some areas you might consider quilting are as follows.

- Quilt in the ditch (that is in the seams between the blocks).
- Echo or contour quilt around motifs, about ¼in (6mm) further out than the edge of the shape.
- Background quilt in a grid or hatched pattern of regularly spaced lines.
- Motif or pattern quilt within blocks or along borders by selecting a specific shape to quilt, such as a heart, bird or paw print.

marking your quilt

If you need to mark a quilting design on your top this can be done before or after you have made the quilt sandwich – most people do it before. There are many marking pens and pencils available but test them on scrap fabric first. If you are machine quilting, marking lines are more easily covered up. For hand quilting you might prefer to use a removable marker or a light pencil. Some water-erasable markers are set by the heat of an iron so take care when pressing.

binding a quilt

Binding a quilt creates a neat and secure edge all round. Binding may be single or double, with double binding being more durable and probably best for bed quilts.

1 Measure your completed quilt top around all edges and add about 8in (20.3cm) extra – this is the length of binding you need. Cut 2½in (6.3cm) wide strips and join them all together to make the length needed. Fold the binding in half along the length and press.

2 Start midway along one side of the quilt and pin the binding along the edge, aligning raw edges. Stitch the binding to the quilt through all layers using a ¼in (6mm) seam until you reach a corner when you should stop ¼in (6mm) away from the end (see Fig 6A).

FIG 6
A

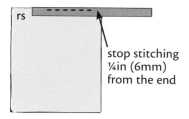

stop stitching ¼in (6mm) from the end

3 Remove the work away from the machine and fold the binding up, northwards, so it is aligned straight with the edge of the quilt (Fig 6B).

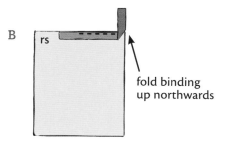

B   rs

fold binding up northwards

4 Hold the corner and fold the binding back down, southwards, aligning it with the raw edge and with the folded corner square. Pin in position and then begin sewing again, from the top and over the fold, continuing down the next edge (Fig 6C). Repeat with the other corners.

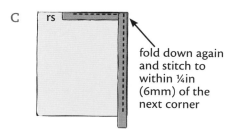

C   rs

fold down again and stitch to within ¼in (6mm) of the next corner

5 When you are nearing the starting point stop 6in (15.2cm) away. Fold back the beginning and end of the binding, so they touch and mark these folds with a pin. Cut the binding ¼in (6mm) from the pin, open out the binding and join with a ¼in (6mm) seam. Press the seam open, re-fold it and slipstitch in place.

6 Fold the binding over to the back of the quilt and slipstitch it in place. Fold the mitres at the corner neatly and secure with tiny slipstitches.

embroidery stitches

I have used various stitches to create the stitcheries on the projects in this book. They are all easy to work and fun to do. Follow these simple diagrams.

blanket stitch

This is my version of this stitch. The conventional method often allows the thread to slip under the edges of the appliqué shape, allowing raw edges to be seen and this method avoids that.

Start at the edge of the appliqué shape, taking needle through to the back of work and come back through to the front of the shape that you are appliquéing a small distance in from the edge where you started. Pull the thread through to form a loop. Put your needle through the loop from front to back, making sure the loop is not twisted. As you pull the thread into place lift the stitch slightly so that it sits on top of the raw edge rather than sliding underneath. Pull the thread firmly into place to avoid loose, floppy stitches. Continue on to make the next stitch.

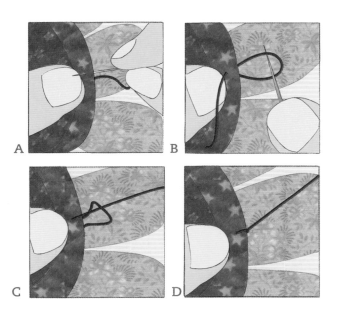

backstitch

Backstitch is an outlining stitch that I also use to 'draw' parts of the design. It is really easy to work and can follow any parts of a design you choose.

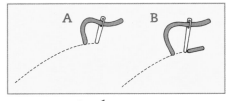

cross stitch

A simple cross stitch is used in many of the stitcheries in the book to add pattern, particularly on dogs' and cats' coats.

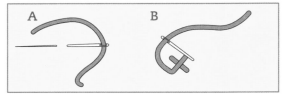

detached chain stitch

Detached chain stitch can be worked in lines and curves or more densely side by side to fill areas of a design. It creates a stronger line visually than backstitch and is good for outlines.

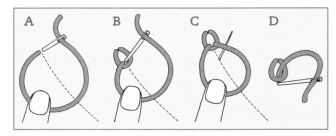

feather stitch

Feather stitch is easy to form and creates a really attractive pattern.

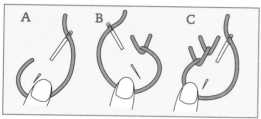

french knot

These little knots are easy to form and are useful for eyes and other details.

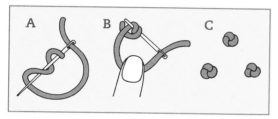

herringbone stitch

Herringbone can be worked to outline areas or form patterns. When stitched in a circle it can create simple flowers.

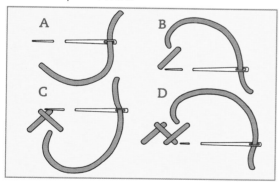

lazy daisy stitch

This decorative stitch is great for flowers especially if the stitches are worked in a circle.

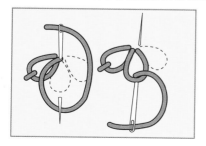

long stitch

Long stitch is just that, a single long stitch. It is useful for coat markings, cat's whiskers and so on.

long and short stitch

This stitch combines a short stitch and a long stitch in an alternating pattern that locks together to create a densely worked area.

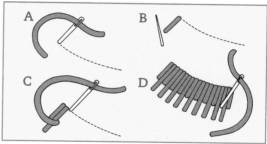

running stitch

These are evenly spaced stitches that can run in any direction or pattern you choose. Quilting stitch is a running stitch.

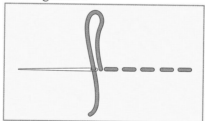

satin stitch

This stitch is an old one that is used to fill in areas of a design with long stitches worked side by side.

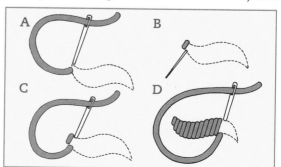

templates

This section contains the stitchery and appliqué templates for the projects. Some templates are reduced to fit the page so read the instructions with each template carefully. Some templates need to have seam allowances added and this is marked on the template. See page 104 for using templates, reversing templates and transferring designs.

puppy dog sewing collection
sewing bag

templates for appliqué (actual size)
add ¼in (6mm) seam allowance to all pieces if using needle-turn appliqué method

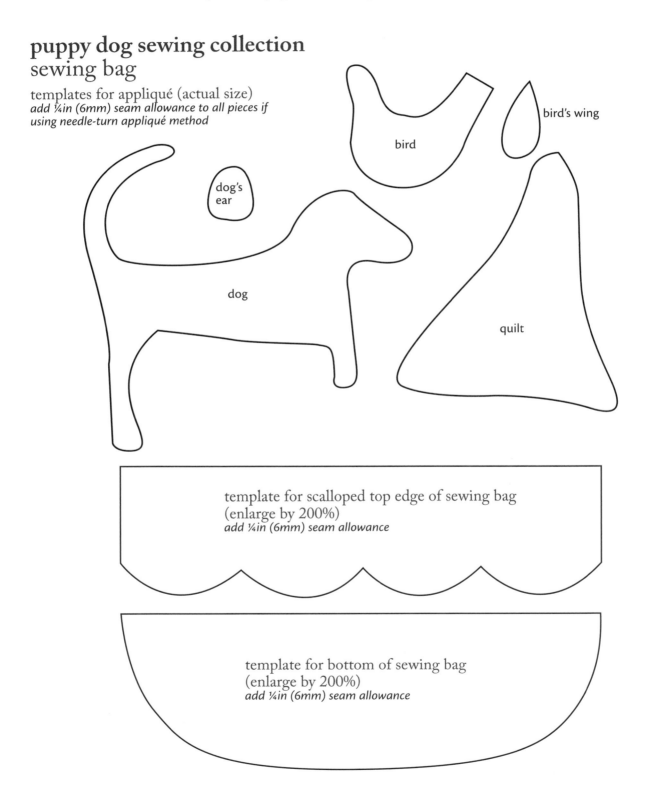

bird

bird's wing

dog's ear

dog

quilt

template for scalloped top edge of sewing bag
(enlarge by 200%)
add ¼in (6mm) seam allowance

template for bottom of sewing bag
(enlarge by 200%)
add ¼in (6mm) seam allowance

sewing bag
stitch pattern
(enlarge by 200% to full size)
the red lines indicate the appliqué areas, showing where surface stitches should be made

scissor keeper

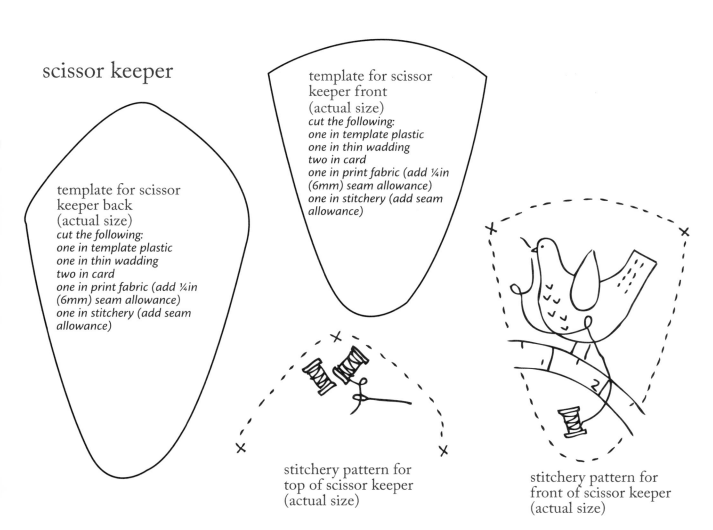

template for scissor
keeper back
(actual size)
*cut the following:
one in template plastic
one in thin wadding
two in card
one in print fabric (add ¼in
(6mm) seam allowance)
one in stitchery (add seam
allowance)*

template for scissor
keeper front
(actual size)
*cut the following:
one in template plastic
one in thin wadding
two in card
one in print fabric (add ¼in
(6mm) seam allowance)
one in stitchery (add seam
allowance)*

stitchery pattern for
top of scissor keeper
(actual size)

stitchery pattern for
front of scissor keeper
(actual size)

needle case

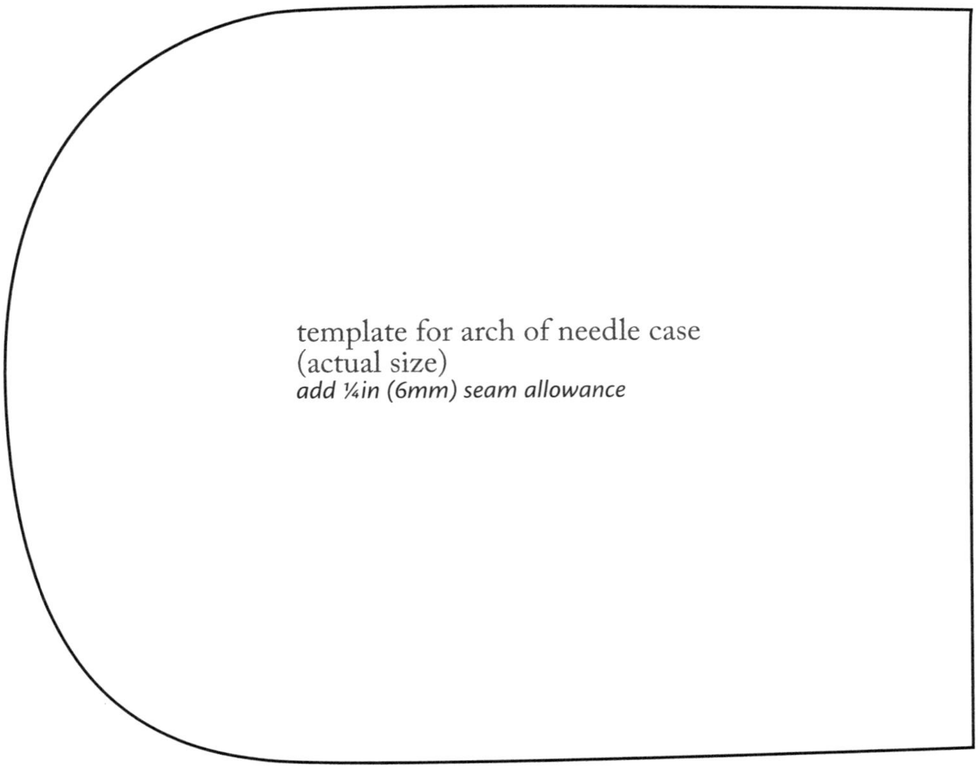

template for arch of needle case
(actual size)
add ¼in (6mm) seam allowance

ABCDEFGHIJKLM
NOPQRSTUVWXYZ
abcdefghijklmnopqrstuvwxyz

alphabet template
(enlarge by 200%)
*use the letters to stitch your
name inside the needle case*

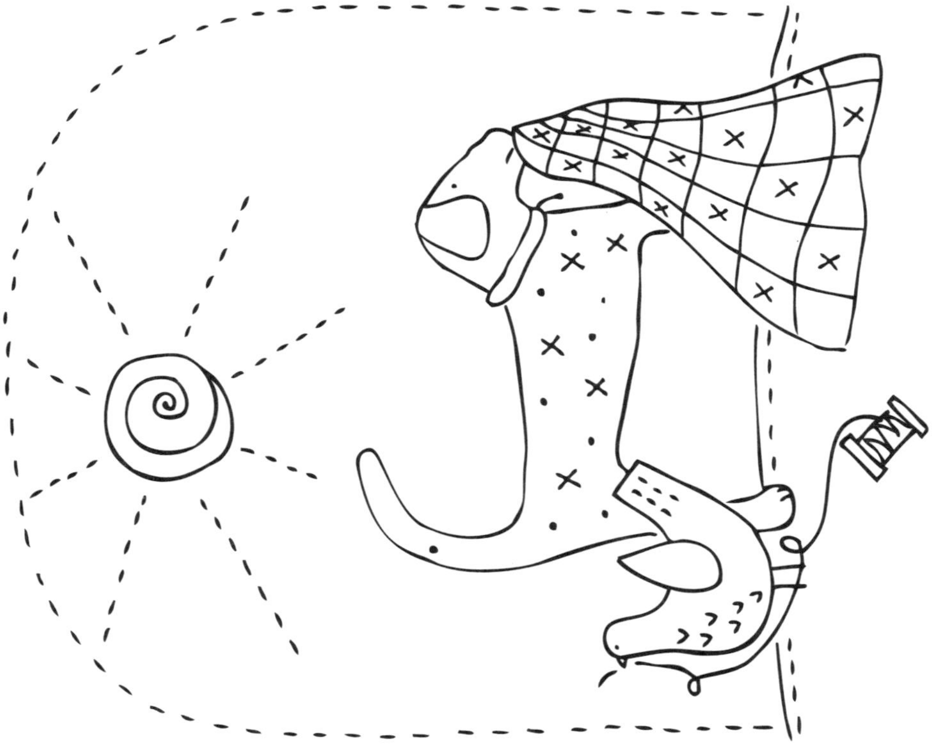

stitch name here

stitchery pattern for front of needle case
(actual size)

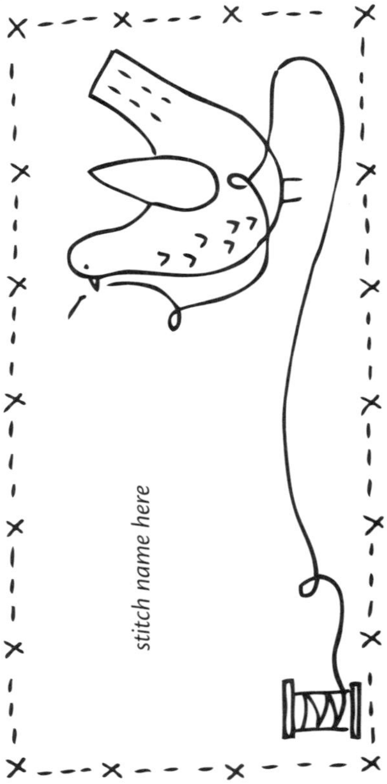

stitch pattern for inside needle case
(actual size)

kitty cat in the garden
bed quilt and journal

stitchery pattern for the meow block (actual size)

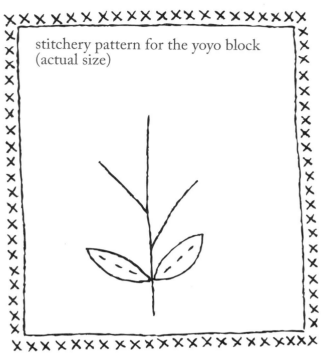

stitchery pattern for the yoyo block
(actual size)

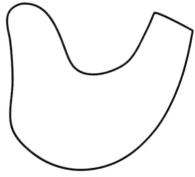

appliqué template for wool bird
(actual size)
no seam allowance needed

template for the yoyo
(actual size)
seam allowance is included

stitchery pattern for cat block
in bed quilt and for journal
(actual size)
*the red lines indicate the appliqué bird
shape and its stitched markings*

woof! woof!
best friend quilt and good boy cushion templates
(enlarge all by 200% to full size)

if using needle-turn appliqué add a ¼in (6mm) seam allowance around all template shapes

– – – – – *indicates position of appliqué shapes on top of main shape*

············ *indicates stitched details*

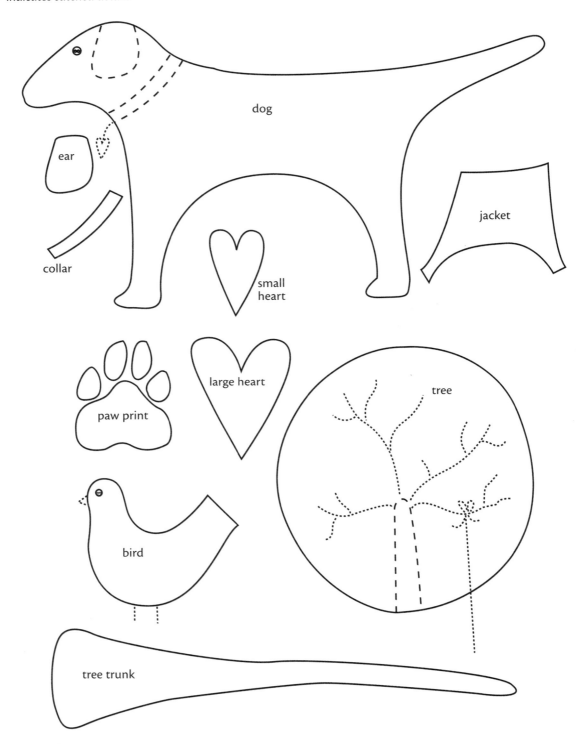

i love my cat
cat lover wall quilt templates
(enlarge all by 200% to full size)
no seam allowances are needed if using fusible web appliqué
– – – – – *indicates position of appliqué shapes on top of main shape*
·········· *indicates stitched details*

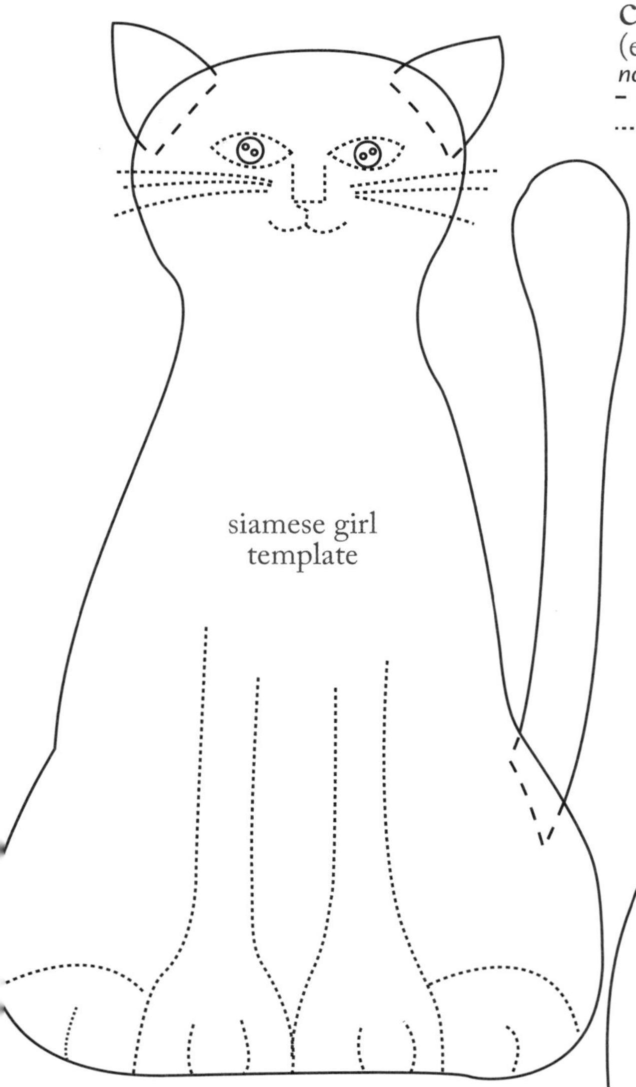

siamese girl template

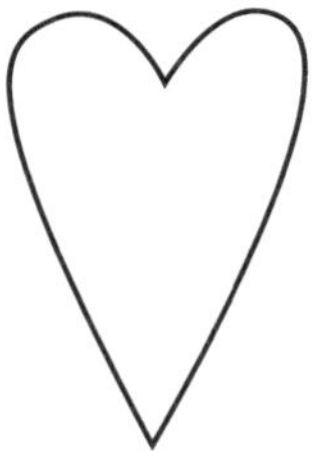

small heart

paw print

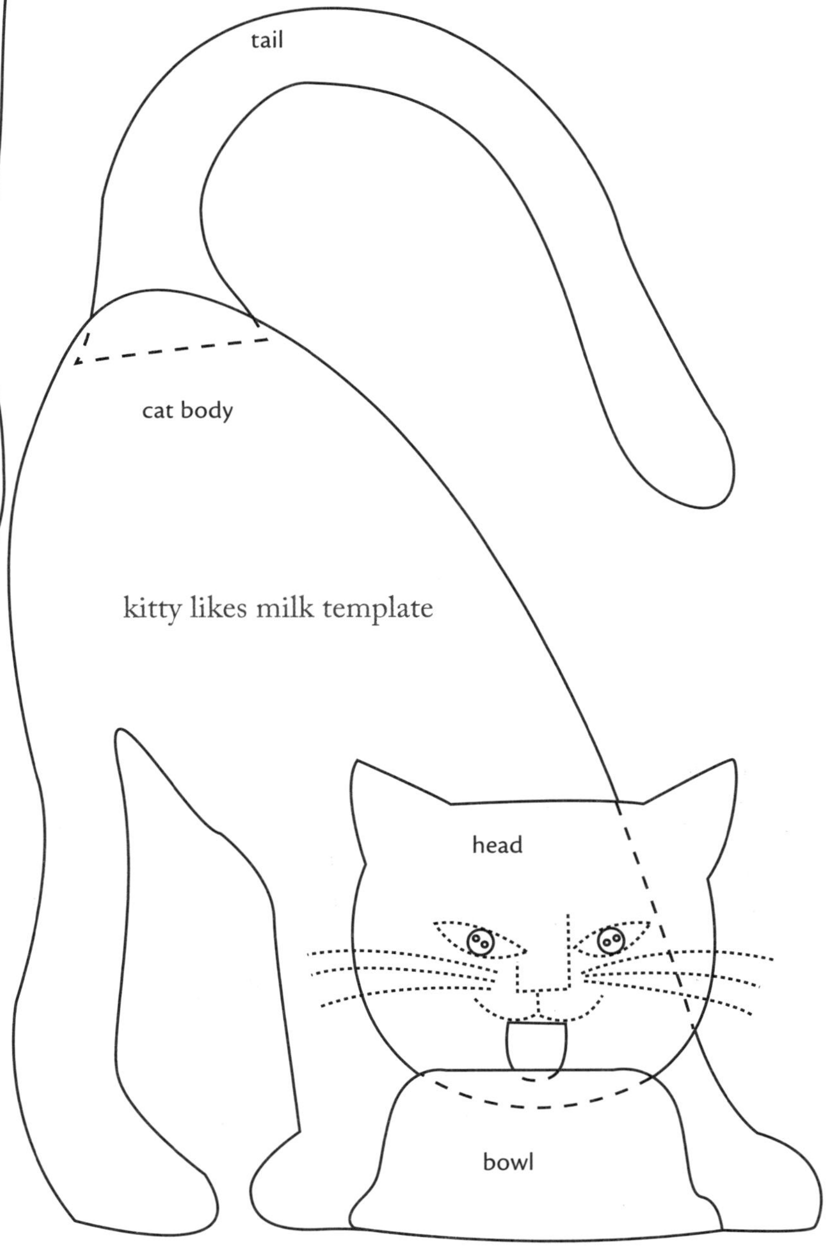

tail

cat body

kitty likes milk template

large heart

head

bowl

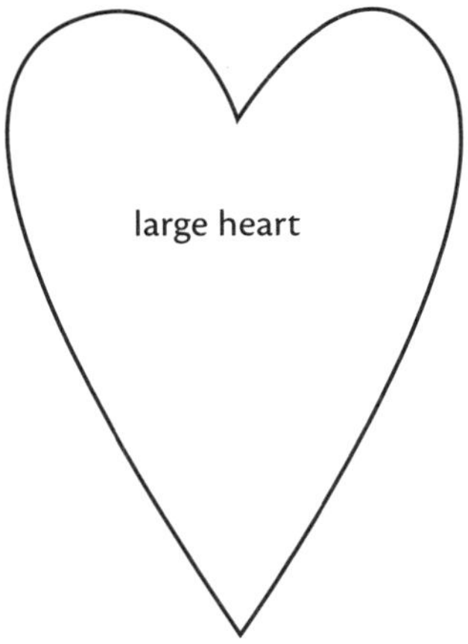

i love my cat
cat lover wall quilt templates
(enlarge template by 200% to full size)
no seam allowances are needed if using fusible web appliqué
– – – – indicates position of appliqué shapes on top of main shape
············ indicates stitched details

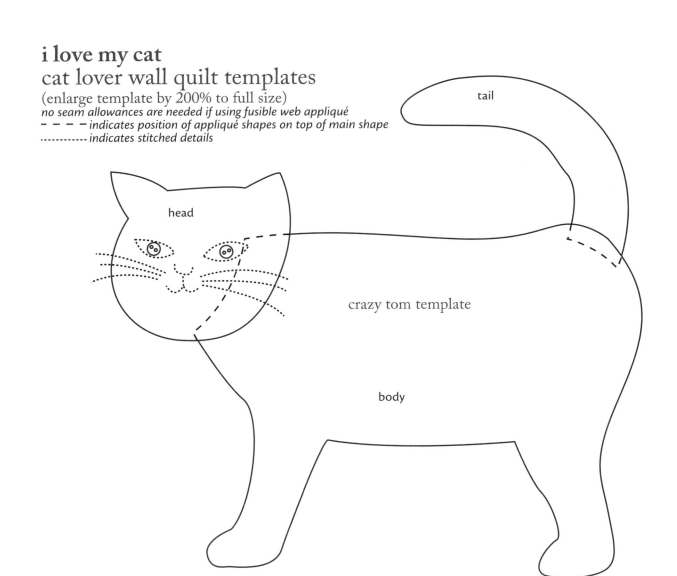

tail

head

crazy tom template

body

purrfect pincushion templates
(enlarge all by 200% to full size)

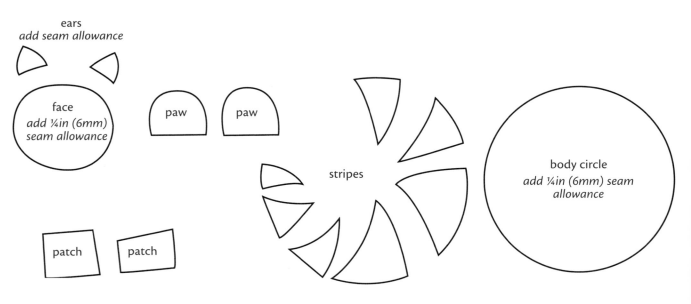

ears
add seam allowance

face
*add ¼in (6mm)
seam allowance*

paw

paw

stripes

body circle
*add ¼in (6mm) seam
allowance*

patch

patch

best of friends
friends hand bag templates
(enlarge all by 400% to full size)
add a ¼in (6mm) seam allowance around all templates

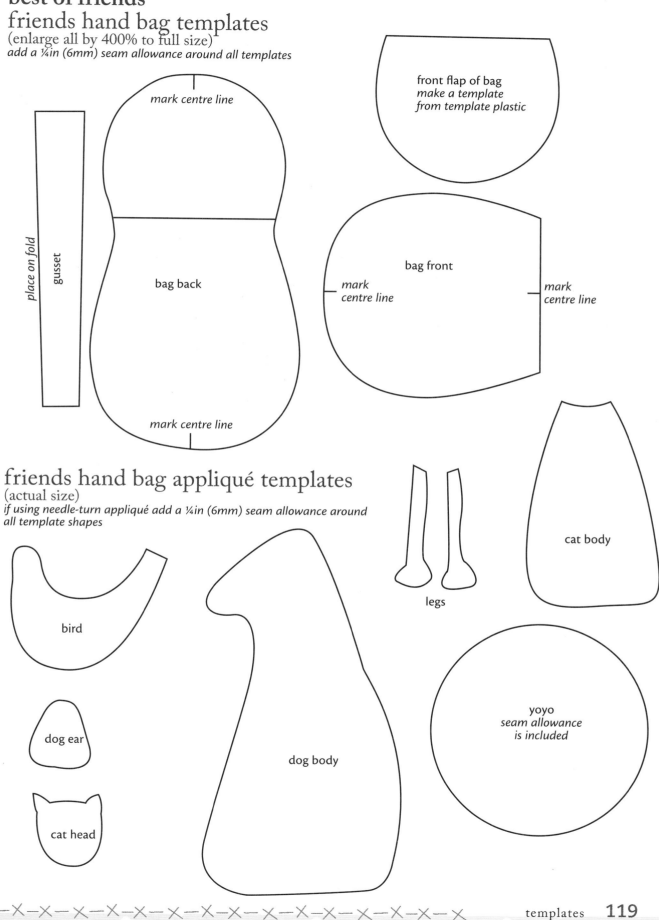

mark centre line

front flap of bag
*make a template
from template plastic*

place on fold

gusset

bag back

bag front

*mark
centre line*

*mark
centre line*

mark centre line

friends hand bag appliqué templates
(actual size)
*if using needle-turn appliqué add a ¼in (6mm) seam allowance around
all template shapes*

bird

legs

cat body

dog ear

dog body

yoyo
*seam allowance
is included*

cat head

best of friends
friends hand bag
stitchery templates
(actual size)

*black lines indicate appliqué;
red lines indicate where the stitchery
for the bag is done after the
appliqué and green lines indicate
stitchery on the base fabric*

little purse
template
(actual size)

A

B

little purse
stitchery template
(actual size)

summer holiday
almost packed
block
stitchery
template A
(actual size)

Follow these steps:
1 Trace Template A on to the background fabric.
2 Use the appliqué templates to do the appliqué.
3 Finally, trace the stitchery design in Template B after the appliqué has been done.

almost packed block
stitchery template B
(actual size)

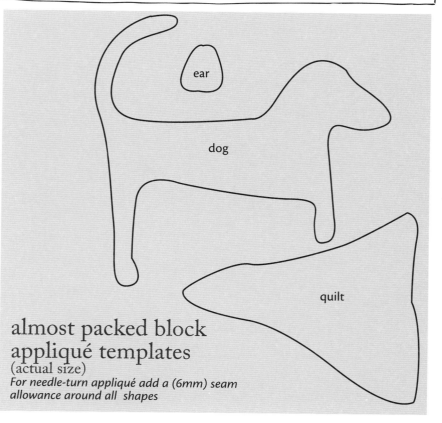

almost packed block
appliqué templates
(actual size)
For needle-turn appliqué add a (6mm) seam allowance around all shapes

ear

dog

quilt

summer holiday
on the road block
stitchery template A
(actual size)

Follow these steps:
1 Trace Template A on to the background fabric.
2 Use the appliqué templates to do the appliqué.
3 Finally, trace the stitchery design in Template B after the appliqué has been done.

on the road block
stitchery template B
(actual size)

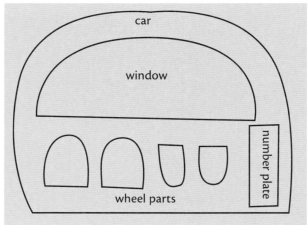

on the road block
appliqué templates
(actual size)
For needle-turn appliqué add a (6mm) seam allowance around all shapes

summer holiday
sunset picnic
blockappliqué template
(actual size)

For needle-turn appliqué add (6mm) seam allowance around shapes

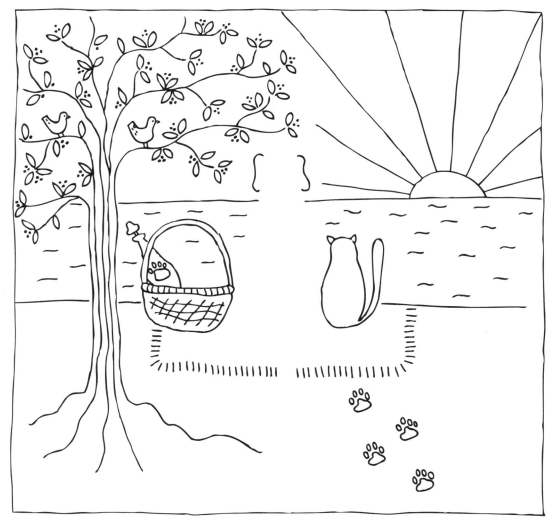

sunset picnic block stitchery template A
(actual size)

Follow these steps:
1 Trace Template A on to the background fabric.
2 Use the appliqué templates to do the appliqué.

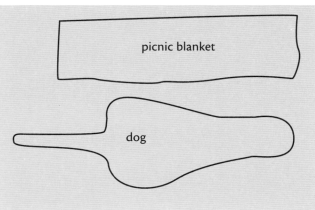

picnic blanket

dog

summer holiday
day at the beach block appliqué templates

(actual size)

*For needle-turn
appliqué add
a (6mm) seam
allowance
around the
shapes*

day at the beach block
stitchery template B
(actual size)

day at the beach block stitchery template A
(actual size)

Follow these steps:
*1 Trace Template A on to the
background fabric.*
*2 Use the appliqué templates
to do the appliqué.*
*3 Finally, trace the stitchery
design in Template B after
the appliqué has been done.*

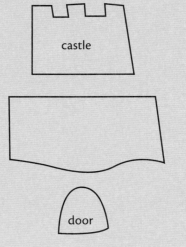

castle

door

summer holiday
at the campsite block stitchery template A
(actual size)

Follow these steps:
1 Trace Template A on to the background fabric.
2 Use the appliqué templates to do the appliqué.
3 Finally, trace the stitchery design in Template B after the appliqué has been done.

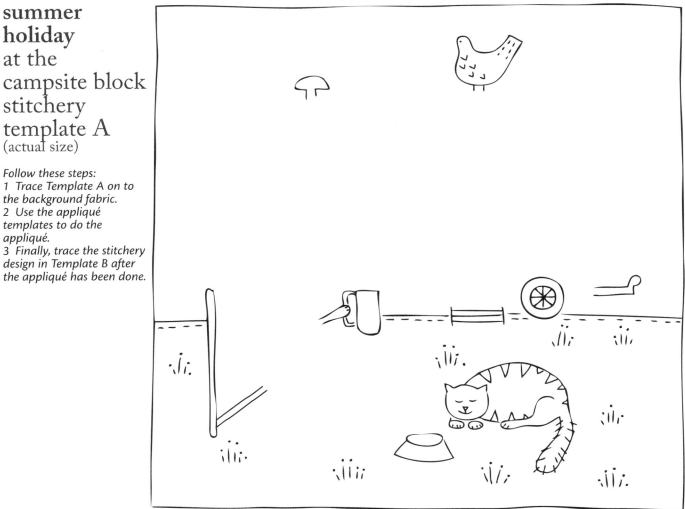

at the campsite block stitchery template B
(actual size)

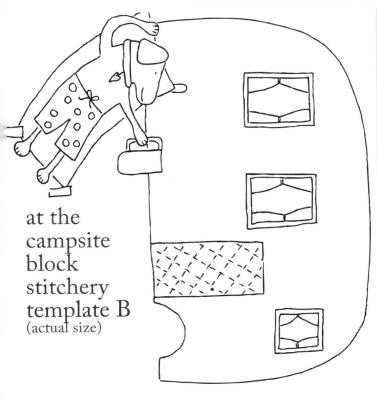

at the campsite block appliqué templates
(actual size)

For needle-turn appliqué add a (6mm) seam allowance around all shapes

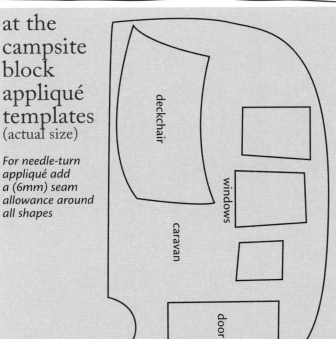

deckchair

caravan

windows

door

forever friends
friends wall hanging template
(actual size)

punch needle box
template
(actual size)

suppliers

Lynette Anderson Designs
PO Box 9314, Pacific Paradise, QLD 4564, Australia
Tel: 07 5450 7497;
from outside Australia +61 5 5450 7497
www.lynetteandersondesigns.com.au
www.lynetteandersondesigns.typepad.com
For all wholesale enquires regarding Lynette's patterns, books and hand-painted wooden buttons

DMC Creative World Ltd
1st Floor Compass Building, Feldspar Close, Enderby, Leicestershire LE19 4SD, UK
Tel: 0116 275 4000
Fax: 0116 275 4020
www.dmccreative.co.uk
www.dmc-usa.com
For embroidery fabrics, stranded cotton, metallic threads and other embroidery supplies

Henry Glass Fabrics
49 West 37th Street, New York, NY 10018, USA
www.henryglassfabrics.com
For fabrics including those from Lynette Anderson Designs

Jo-Ann Stores Inc
5555 Darrow Road, Hudson, Ohio, USA
Tel: 1 888 739 4120
Email: guest service@jo-annstores.com
www.joann.com
For craft, needlework and quilting supplies, including weaver's cloth (mail order and shops across US)

Patchwork with Busyfingers
PO Box 433, Eumundi QLD 4562, Australia
Tel: 07 5442 7818;
from outside Australia +61 7 5442 7818
www.busyfingerspatchwork.com
For equilateral triangles and corners for English paper piecing (wholesale and retail).

about the author

Lynette Anderson's love affair with textiles began at a young age when her grandmother taught her to embroider and knit. Patchwork caught Lynette's attention in 1981 after the birth of her first son, and her affinity with textiles is apparent in her work. Moving with her family to Australia in 1990 prompted the release of Lynette first patterns in 1995 and during the ensuing years she has produced hundreds of patterns. Lynette's distinctive, yet sophisticated naïve design style encompasses quilts, pillows, bags and sewing accessories. Her popular self-published books include, *Bearly Stitched, Sunflower Stitching, An Angel's Wish, Friends For Christmas* and *Rainbow Cottage*. Lynette was very excited when she was asked to join the team at Henry Glass Fabrics and launched her first fabric lines in 2009. Visit Lynette at www.lynetteandersondesigns.typepad.com

acknowledgments

Many thanks to Val and Christine who helped me with the hand embroidery, to Debbie St Germain for her punch needle skills and to Belinda Betts and Elizabeth Traynor for enhancing the quilts with their wonderful machine quilting.

index

ageing work 94, 99
alphabet template 114
appliqué 105
fusible web 105
needle-turn 105

bed quilts 26–33, 38–45, 116
bindings 33, 50, 109
borders 32, 45, 59–60, 87, 90, 93, 107
boxes 94–5, 100–1, 126
buttons 44, 50, 68, 102

cords 25
craft glue 103
crazy patchwork 68, 71, 105–6
cushions 38–9, 46–51, 116
cutters 103

English paper piecing 106

fabrics 102
flowers, yo-yo 26–8, 34, 68, 70, 107, 115
fusible web/interfacing 102

handbags 66–73, 119–20
handles, bag 17
hearts 43, 49, 58–9, 90, 116–17

ironing 104

joining strips 108
journals 26–7, 34–7

lap quilts 78–90, 121–5
light boxes 103

marking quilts 103, 109

needle cases 7, 10–13, 18–21, 114
needles 103
nine-patch blocks 78, 88

painting 52, 58, 103
paws 43, 49, 60, 116–17
photo albums 78, 91–3
pincushions 52, 62–5, 118
pins 103
pockets 20
punch needle work 94–101, 103, 106
purses 66, 74–7, 120

quilting 33, 45, 49–50, 61, 90, 108

ric-rac braid 26, 37

scissor keepers 7, 10–13, 22–5, 113
seam sewing 104
sewing bags 7, 10–17, 112–13
star blocks 40–2, 46–7
stitch types 110–11
straps 72–3

tassels 25
tea-dyeing 57, 104
templates 103–4, 112–26
threads 102
transferring designs 104
trees 43–4, 49, 116, 122–3

wadding (batting) 102
wall quilts 52–61, 94–9, 117–18, 126